GEMSTONES

UNDERSTANDING   IDENTIFYING   BUYING

GEMSTONES

UNDERSTANDING   IDENTIFYING   BUYING

KEITH WALLIS FGA

ANTIQUE COLLECTORS' CLUB

© 2006 Keith Wallis

World copyright reserved

ISBN 10: 1-851-49-494-4
ISBN 13: 978-1-85149-494-1

The right of Keith Wallis to be identified as author of this work has been asserted by him in accordance with the Copyright, Designs and Patents Act 1988

Frontispiece:
Brooch set with opal, diamond and demantoid garnets, see page 51. (Photo: WL)

Title page:
CZ model of the Williamson diamond, a pure pink diamond weighing 236cts. One of the finest for its quality and unusual colour, it was presented to Princess Elizabeth on her wedding day in 1947 by Dr. John T. Williams. Shown actual size. (Photo: RH)

British Library Cataloguing-in-Publication Data
A catalogue record for this book is available from the British Library

Printed in China
Published in England by the Antique Collectors' Club Ltd., Woodbridge, Suffolk

Contents

CONTENTS

Acknowledgements

The Author wishes to thank the following for their kind help and assistance:

L. Allen Brown GIA
Alan Clark FGA, DGA
Creetown Museum
Terry Davidson FGA
Gem-A
Dr Roger Harding BSc, DPhil, FGA
Alan Hodgkinson FGA, DGA
Roy Huddlestone
E Alan Jobbins BSc, FGA

Marcus McCullam
Geoffrey Munn, Wartski, London
Bonnie Pemberton GIT, GG, AJP
Peter Read CEng, MIEE, MIERE, FGA, FISTC
Michele Rowan
Tim Stephenson FGA
True North Gems Inc.
Colin Winter FGA, DGA

Photographs supplied by:-

Chris Algar	(CA)
All That Glitters	(ATG)
Antique Collectors' Club	(ACC)
Sabine Betts	(SB)
Maggie Campbell Pederson	(MCP)
Chatham Created Gems	(Chatham)
Christie's Images	(Christie's)
Diamond Trading Corporation	(DTC)
Gem-A	(Gem-A)
Juliet Henney	(JH)
Alan Hodgkinson	(AH)
Huddlestone Gemmological Consultants	(RH)
Alan Jobbins	(AJ)
Korite – Canada	(Korite)
Marcus McCullam	(MM)
Geoffrey Munn, Wartski, London	(WL)
Natural History Museum	(NHM)
Michele Rowan	(MR)
True North Gems Inc.	(TNG)
Douglas Unwin, Creetown Museum	(DU)
Keith Wallis	(KW)
Wartski, London	(WL)
Colin Winter	(CW)

Please note that unless otherwise stated, gems are shown larger than actual size.

Foreword

Until I discovered gemmology in my twenties, my appreciation of gemstones was simple. Like most young women, in a jeweller's I became like a young girl in a sweet shop, dazzled by the glittering colourful assortment under the glass counter and agonising over the choice. A gem's beauty was enough to captivate me. But to study the science and history behind these fascinating specimens that emerge from our earth is to enter a whole new world of sweet shops where you quickly learn that red does not always mean strawberry flavour and yellow is not necessarily lemon. The experience is surprising and may help you avoid a bad taste in your mouth when buying.

This book will encourage the budding enthusiast not only to look, but to handle and, ultimately, identify gems. Those previously afraid to touch will be taught to proceed with caution and lured further into exploring the fascinating gem minefields of today. Not only do these pages provide a good preliminary study of the major gemstones one might encounter, including recognisable features for those with little handling experience and tests to try in identification, but it gently introduces the complex factors and properties that occupy gemmologists worldwide, from pleochroism and 'fluorescence' to 'specific gravity' and 'refraction'. The complexities of science are stripped to a basic framework on which the reader may build a comprehensive understanding of gems. The reader is steered through history and mystery, science and

beliefs, 'naturals' and synthetics, treatments and simulants, highlighting the pitfalls and perils that beset the collector and investor alike in the real world.

For the traveller who is keen to try his hand at buying stones abroad, there are useful tips on what to look for in specific locations: well kept secrets, like the 'Amber Valley' in the Dominican Republic are juxtaposed with clear warnings such as the illicit trading in black coral in the West Indies and the local Thai 'businessmen' who prey on unsuspecting tourists; the names of popular stones are translated into four European languages as an appendix to help you navigate foreign markets. Not only will you be better equipped when you arrive in distant parts but your increased awareness will undoubtedly empower your bargaining skills!

If you prefer to stay safely in your armchair, the list of informative websites and suggestions for further reading provide a spring board from which you may deepen your interest and understanding. At the very least, I hope you will find it a little easier when buying, to choose.

Kate Bliss BA Hons (Oxon) MRICS FGA

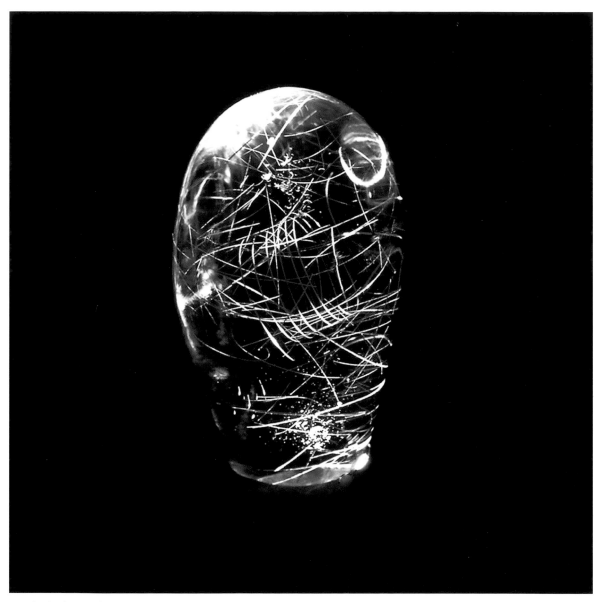

Inclusions of other minerals are sometimes seen in stones and are used by the gemmologist to identify certain gems. The leading authority on inclusions was the late Edward Gubelin; his many books of photographs taken under the microscope display nature's art in a most astounding manner. This photo of rock crystal shows how amazing and complex inclusions can be. This example, which is actually 56mm x 33mm (2⅕ x 1⅓in), is extremely rare. (Photo: AJ)

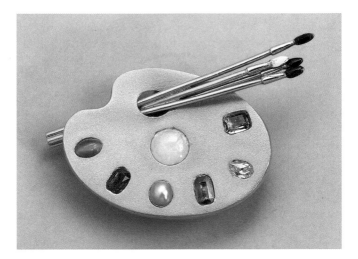

Gold brooch in the form of an artist's palette; set with a chrysoberyl cat's eye, a ruby, pearl, sapphire, diamond, emerald and an opal. (Photo: WL)

Introduction

Most women possess a gemstone and, if they are lucky, several, whether in brooches, rings or necklaces. Men also occasionally sport a diamond ring or tie pin and these days even a diamond stud in their ear.

But what do these stones mean to the wearer? A token of affection, an heirloom, or something that glitters and looks attractive? Perhaps it is an open display of wealth, or something to keep locked away in a bank vault as an investment. The gemstone can mean many things to the owner.

There are literally hundreds of different gemstones, but only the most important are covered in this book. Some beautiful gems are simply so rare or too fragile to be worn as jewellery that they are only bought by collectors; these are known as collectors' stones. In fact there are new gems being discovered almost every year; if not a new species, then a different colour of a known stone.

WHAT CONSTITUTES A GEMSTONE?

If the stones you are wearing are natural, then, with a few minor exceptions, they will have been created millions of years ago. Formed in the depths of the earth under great heat and pressure, they were pushed to the surface by erupting volcanoes, often being washed out of the rocks by water into rivers where they can now be recovered. Others have to be mined, like coal, from many metres under the ground. These rough stones are then sold to local dealers, who either sell them on, via agents, to the major dealers or have them cut locally (native cut). The better stones end up in the cutting rooms of Israel, Holland, Belgium, USA or Germany. There the full beauty of the stone is revealed.

To be classed as a gemstone the crystal has to fulfil three parameters: beauty, durability and rarity.

Many gems fulfil these parameters to differing degrees. Diamond, for instance, is the most durable of stones due to it's great hardness, but hit one with a hammer and it will shatter, so it is not the toughest; toughness and hardness being two different things. As you are unlikely to hit your precious diamond with a hammer, this distinction is not too important. It was, however, put to dubious use by some of the early diamond dealers: prospectors would bring in stones to sell to the dealers, who recognising the gems as genuine, would hit one stone with a rock, thus shattering it, and demonstrating to the gullible seller that they were obviously not real diamonds as real ones were 'hard'. The dealers then bought the remaining diamonds for a pittance. Diamond is without doubt very beautiful, but are they rare? Well, not really, but we'll discuss this question later on.

Ruby is the next hardest of the gemstones and the best examples can be more rare than diamonds. Emerald, in its best quality, even more so, but it is far less durable. (see Tables 1 & 2)

Rough gems, clockwise from top left: emerald, sapphire, garnet, rhodonite, tourmaline and apatite. Durable and rare, but not yet beautiful. (Photo: KW)

Together with sapphire, these stones constitute the so-called four 'precious stones'. Note that ruby and sapphire are actually both corundum, but of different colour.

Ruby and diamond catherine wheel with enamel fuse, English, c.1900. (Photo: WL)

Diamonds – beautiful even in their rough form.
(Photo: AH)

All other gemstones have been classed as semi-precious. A strange differentiation, but that has been the accepted classification for many years. Consequently such beautiful stones as tourmaline, zircon, peridot, topaz, aquamarine, alexandrite and amethyst, to name but a few, were called semi-precious. Fortunately times have changed and most gems are now classed as 'precious'.

The Mohs scale is based on a simple test: which stone will scratch the one of a lower number? This is classed as 'destructive testing', which is generally frowned upon by gemmologists. Destructive tests may be used when checking pieces of rough mineral – but gem materials? Never! The right-hand column of Table 1 shows the Knoop scale – a more accurate scale of hardness, based on testing by indentation.

Note how much harder diamond is to other gems: nearly 3 times harder than moissanite and six times harder than cubic zirconia according to the Knoop Scale. A hardness of '7' on the Mohs scale is normally taken as the minimum for acceptable stones to use in jewellery. As can be seen from Table 1, certain gems, such as amber, pearl and turquoise, are softer than this and still used in jewellery, though care must be taken when wearing such gems

Table 1 Mohs Scale of Hardness

Stone	Mohs	Knoop
Talc	1	12.3
Gypsum	2	61
Amber	2 – 2.5	
Calcite	3	141
Pearl	2.5 – 3.5	
Fluorite & Malachite	4	181
Apatite	5	483
Turquoise, Glass & Strontium Titanate	5.5 – 6	
Feldspar, Opal (average)	6	621
Peridot, Demantoid Garnet & GGG	6.5 – 7	
Quartz (Amethyst, Citrine, Cairngorm) & Jadeite	7	788
Zircon, Tourmaline, Garnet	7.5	
Emerald	7.5 – 8	
Topaz, Spinel	8	1190
Chrysoberyl, Cubic Zirconia & YAG	8.5	1400
Corundum (Ruby & **Sapphire**)	9	2200
Moissanite	9.25	3000
Diamond	10	8200

*The ten stones shown in **bold** were in the original Mohs scale; the other stones have been added for interest.*

Table 2 Mohs scale of hardness: everyday materials

Everyday item	**Mohs**
Finger nail	2.5
Copper coin	3
Window glass	5.5
Knife blade	6
Steel file	6.5

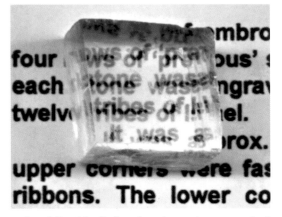

Example of Double Refraction through a crystal of calcite. (Photo KW)

TECHNICAL TERMS

(I must stress that these are simplistic definitions but adequate for the purposes of this book.)

Specific Gravity or *density* – The S.G. (specific gravity) of a gemstone refers to its weight in air compared to the weight of an equal volume of water. What this means is that the higher the S.G. of a stone the heavier it will weigh compared to gems of a lower S.G. Consequently a one carat diamond (S.G. 3.51) is smaller in size than a one carat tourmaline (S.G. 3.00) because the diamond is denser than the tourmaline. So, the higher the S.G. the smaller the stone of an equivalent weight.

Refraction and *Refractive index* – When a ray of light passes from one medium into another it is bent. Stand a stick in a glass of water, making sure a portion of the stick is above the water level. You will see that at the point it is immersed in the water it appears to bend. This is refraction. The same thing occurs when light enters a gemstone.

The specific angle at which the light bends varies between different gems. This is measured and is interpreted into the *refractive index* for that stone. Gemstones fall into two different categories as regards refraction: the singly refractive and the doubly refractive. This depends on the crystal system to which they belong; there are seven systems, only one, the cubic is singly refractive; all the rest are double. Double refraction means that the stone splits the light ray into two and each ray has a different angle so the stone has two refractive indices. Some doubly refractive stones also have a property called dichroism. This means that, when viewed from two different directions, the stone appears a different colour or shade in each. There are many examples – ruby (yellowish-red and deep red), blue sapphire (pale greenish-blue and deep blue) are just two. Certain gems are pleochroic – showing three different colours or shades depending on the direction viewed. Gemmologists use a refractometer to establish the refractive index of a gem.

BASIC GEMMOLOGISTS' INSTRUMENTS

Loupe – A lens of ten times magnification, the loupe is the gemmologist's most important aid in the inspection and identification of precious stones. It is the tool used to decide the clarity of a diamond. If an inclusion or other imperfection cannot be seen through the loupe, it is classed as 'flawless' or 'loupe clean'. This is a world standard for diamonds. The best type is called a triplet as, when used correctly, this gives the best possible image.

To use the loupe, first hold the stone using tongs or tweezers, preferably black. This will need a bit of practice so that a valuable stone does not flick out and get lost – this is particularly embarrassing if you happen to be in a shop at the time! Luckily loupes are available with a slide lock to hold the gem firm, either way it is a good idea to try it out on something of low value first. An alternative that holds the stone very firmly is the four claw stone holder. None of these items need be very expensive; a perfectly good loupe can be bought for about £16, a pair of tongs from £12. Now hold the loupe close to your eye and move the gem up towards it until the gem is in focus. Try to keep both eyes open; it is less

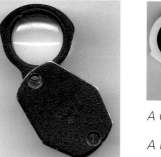

A Chelsea Filter. (Photo: KW)

A loupe. (Photo: KW)

The author using a Chelsea Filter. (Photo: JP)

The author using a loupe. (Photo: JP)

tiring and an easy thing to do with a little practice. Remember to look at the gem from all directions not just through the table and take your time, some flaws take a bit of finding.

The loupe can provide pleasure by exploring the surface of a mineralised rock under a strong light and discovering tiny crystals hiding in the crevices. Try it!

Chelsea Colour Filter – This was developed in the early 1930s at the London Chamber of Commerce's Gem Testing Laboratory together with the Chelsea College of Science and Technology. It was designed to combat the increase in the number of emerald simulants coming on to the market.

It consists of a sandwich of a couple of filters that only transmit deep red and yellow-green light. This instrument was able to distinguish the real stone from the then common glass, fakes and doublets. The true emerald (with a few rare exceptions) appear red or pinkish when viewed in strong light under the filter, the simulants show green. Unfortunately synthetic emeralds such as Gilson and Chatham also show red, but this tends to be a brighter red. (Other uses for this filter are detailed under each particular stone where applicable.)

To use the filter shine a strong artificial light on to the stone and view the illuminated stone through the filter. A Chelsea Colour Filter will cost you about £20. Both the instruments described here may be purchased from:

Gem-A Instruments Ltd.

27 Greville St. London EC1N 8TN.

History, Myths and Legends

Since caveman, men and women have been decorating themselves with whatever was to hand: paint, bone ornaments and clay beads. The use of pretty stones dates back to the Ancient Egyptians, the Ancient Greeks and the Romans. Emerald was being mined in Egypt many thousand of years ago and simulants soon followed in the form of glass. The Greeks were engraving *intaglios* from serpentine back in 600BC and wearing them as rings to use as seals. Gemstones were certainly collected and valued, though they did not have the appearance that we are used to today as the art of faceting did not come into its own until the Middle Ages. Instead of being 'cut', stones were ground into cabochons. Often these cabochons would also be engraved using diamonds as etching tools. Diamonds were also used decoratively, but due to the lack of the necessary skills required to make the most of their brilliance, they would have been dull compared with those of today. Later, the prized octahedral crystals were mounted into rings in their natural state.

Those of you who know your Bible will know that a number of gemstones are mentioned. For example, in the Old Testament, there is a description of the Jewish High Priest's breastplate, set with gems in four rows of three, each stone having the name of a tribe engraved upon it. Some of the names of the gems are rather odd, however, and not readily recognised as those that we know today.

Diamond octahedron. (Photo: RH)

Table 3 Breastplate of the High Priest

Made of embroidered cloth, it was set with four rows of 'precious' stones, three in each row. On each stone was engraved the name of one of the twelve tribes of Israel.
It was approximately 10 inches square; the two upper corners were fastened to the ephod by blue ribbons. The lower corners were fastened to the priest's girdle.
It was also known as 'The Breastplate of Judgement'.

The first row shall be a sardius, a topaz and a carbuncle
The second row shall be an emerald, a sapphire and a diamond
The third row shall be a ligure, an agate and an amethyst
The fourth row shall be a beryl, an onyx and a jasper
They shall be set in gold.
        (Abbreviated from Exodus 28: 17-20, King James Version)

Another translation by Jerome and the Septuagint gives:
1st row – sardius (carnelian), topazius (peridot), smaragdus (green stone)
2nd row – carbuncle (ruby or garnet), sapphire (lapis lazuli), jasper
3rd row – ligurius (amber), achates (agate), amerthystus (amethyst)
4th row – chrysolitus (citrine), beryllion (beryl), onychion (onyx)

MYTHS AND LEGENDS

There are a myriad of tales to tell about what people believed, and in fact still believe, about the properties of various stones. From the early days gemstones were regarded as having special powers: they were used as talismans and believed to be able to make the wearer invincible and even, in some cases, invisible. Others protected against the evil eye and magic spells. Engraved stones became highly prized and were considered as more potent in their power than plain stones.

The alchemists of the Middle Ages allocated curative properties to gemstones, vaguely similar to homeopathic medicine today.

Certain stones, for instance topaz, were attributed with the ability to cool water and consequently when

Philip II of Spain (after Titian). (Photo: KW)

Table 4 Qualities Bestowed on Gemstones

Star Signs	Properties	Class
Aries, Leo and Sagittarius	Hot & Dry	Fire
Taurus, Virgo and Capricorn	Cold & Dry	Earth
Gemini, Libra and Aquarius	Hot & Moist	Air
Cancer, Scorpio and Pisces	Cold & Moist	Water

powdered and added to wine were believed to reduce fevers. Green stones were thought to help poor eyesight, yellow to treat jaundice. Amethyst was supposed to ensure sobriety, because of this, Bishops of the Anglican Church have worn amethyst rings ever since the Reformation.

The diseases of the time were classified according to a system of four qualities – hot, cold, moist or dry – and the stones used to treat them had the appropriate qualities. Stones considered hot and dry would, for instance, be used to treat a case of dropsy, which was thought to stem from cold, moist sources.

If the patient were rich, he might even be given a cocktail of crushed gems. Indeed, Philip II of Spain was given what was called the Most Noble Electuary of Jacinth, consisting of powdered 'jacinth' (zircon or spinel), emerald, sapphire, topaz, pearl and red coral,

together with twenty-two other animal and vegetable ingredients. Philip died two days later.

Gemstones also played a part in astrology; we have all heard of birthstones – these in fact developed from the stones of the High Priest's breastplate, mentioned earlier.

The astrological divisions were based on the dates of the equinoxes (i.e. the days that the sun crosses the equator), on approximately 21 March and 23 September. The heavens were mapped out with constellations symbolised by mythological figures and animals; those in the belt along which the sun made its daily course were collectively called the zodiac. The earliest lists allied gemstones to the signs of the zodiac. These were later related to each month of the year. The list of stones does not remain static and new stones are added from time to time; lists may also vary from dealer to dealer. Stones were also allocated to each planet and even to days of the week, many of these associations have stayed with us in our modern culture, the association of gemstones and precious metals with anniversaries, for example.

PROPERTIES ASSOCIATED WITH GEMS

Diamond – As the 'King of Gems' to the pearl's 'Queen', it is naturally endowed with every good and noble characteristic. The diamond was thought to bring victory to the wearer, giving him superior strength, fortitude and courage. Associated with thunder and lightning, it was believed that diamond could even be consumed or melted by a thunderbolt. Diamond was also believed to indicate guilt or innocence, the stone growing dim if the accused was guilty and shining brightly if he was innocent. Another curious belief was that diamonds were supposed to possess reproductive powers. This idea was also applied to other gems.

Amethyst – This gem has probably the widest range of miraculous powers of any of the precious stones. As was said earlier it was believed to prevent drunkenness and was therefore set in Bishops' rings. It also possessed the power of inducing dreams and visions. Leonardo da Vinci believed that it could dispel evil thoughts and quicken intelligence. It was imbued with the power to protect farmers' fields from storms and locusts, to bring good luck in war and hunting. It was even believed to protect against snake bites.

Aquamarine – This stone would be placed in a glass of water as a remedy against eye trouble, toothache, sore throat, liver problems, glandular swellings and feelings of weakness. It was thought to promote a happy marriage, but was also considered to be advantageous in avoiding discovery in the event of infidelity. Aquamarine, when ground into flat plates, could enhance the clarity of view and was reported to have been made into spectacles in the 14th century.

Emerald – This gem was reputed to cure blindness; Nero was said to have had a monocle made of emerald. It was believed to preserve the chastity of women, which, if violated, would cause the stone to burst in to fragments. Emerald was also supposed to blind poisonous snakes. It is a highly-prized stone for Muslims, as green is the sacred colour of the Prophet. In Asian countries it represents hopes of immortality, courage and exalted faith.

Opal – Myth and legend describe opal as 'Cupid's Stone of hope and love'. It was held in the greatest esteem as it contained the red of the ruby, the blue of the sapphire, the green of emerald, the gold of topaz, and the purple of the amethyst; thus it was imbued with the properties of all these stones. Only emerald was held in higher esteem. Many people over the centuries believed this gem to bring good luck. In the western world, however, it gained the reputation of being unlucky in the nineteenth century after the publication of Sir Walter Scott's novel Anne of Geierstein, in which the heroine wears a cursed opal in her hair, and later dies.

Peridot – This was the favourite stone of the pirates as they believed that it would protect them against all forms of evil and, if set in gold, would save them from the terrors of the night. It was supposed to strengthen eyesight, as well as the heart and respiratory tract. It was also supposed to relieve depression and even protect against baldness.

Ruby – Believed to be an antidote for poison, this gem was also attributed with prophetic powers, the stone apparently darkening to warn of impending danger. In Roman time, rubies from Greece engraved with dragons or dogs were especially prized. The gem is also extolled by Hindus as ensuring health, wealth and a joyous nature to the owner.

Sapphire – This gem symbolises truth, sincerity and faithfulness. It also was believed to have curative properties and to keep one safe from illness and protect against poison and spells. It was also associated with religious rites and ceremonies of the Christian Church. Sapphire-set rings are worn by Bishops and Cardinals of the Roman Catholic Church. In the Middle Ages sapphire was worn as a talisman to cure ophthalmic disorders; later it was used as a test for female virtue.

Turquoise – Used since ancient times as a talisman against falling from horseback by Mongolians who attached this stone to their horses' bridles, it became a protection from all kinds of fall. Arabs, who still paint the doors of their houses blue, also wore it as a protection against the evil eye. It was also popular with couples getting engaged, with pregnant women and for newborn babies.

Table 5 Stones associated with the Zodiac

Star Sign	Gemstone
Aries	Diamond
Taurus	Emerald or Chrysoprase
Gemini	Pearl or Moonstone
Cancer	Ruby or Carnelian
Leo	Sardonyx or Peridot
Virgo	Sapphire or Lapis Lazuli
Libra	Opal or Tourmaline
Scorpio	Topaz
Sagittarius	Turquoise or Zircon
Capricorn	Garnet
Aquarius	Amethyst
Pisces	Aquamarine or Bloodstone

Table 6 Indian Planetary Stones

Planet	Gem
Sun	Ruby
Moon	Pearl
Mars	Coral
Mercury	Emerald
Jupiter	Yellow Sapphire
Venus	Diamond
Saturn	Blue Sapphire
Rahu (Moon's north node)	Hessonite Garnet
Ketu (Moon's south node)	Cat's Eye

Navaratna jewels are made using all the Indian planetary gems together in a single jewel.

Table 7 Stones Related to the Days of the Week

Day	Gemstone
Sunday	Pearl
Monday	Emerald
Tuesday	Topaz
Wednesday	Turquoise
Thursday	Sapphire
Friday	Ruby
Saturday	Amethyst

Table 8 Anniversary Stones

Anniversary	Gem
Thirtieth	Pearl
Thirty-fifth	Coral
Fortieth	Ruby
Forty-fifth	Sapphire
Fiftieth	Gold
Fifty-fifth	Emerald
Sixtieth	Diamond

Superstition and magical powers are given to gemstones even today, as you can discover by visiting one of the many Gemshows that are currently popular. Crystal pendulums are produced to be worn around the neck for a variety of purposes. These are usually quartz and sometimes referred to as 'points'. They are used in different ways: dangling the point over the abdomen of a pregnant mother, for instance, is supposed to reveal the sex of the unborn child, according to the direction in which the crystal rotates.

It is also claimed that crystals can heal physical ailments by the appropriate gem being applied to the seven 'Chakra' points along the spinal column from the top of the head to the base of the spine.

All that a gemmologist can say is that quartz does have certain strange qualities. If a thin section is put under tension, radio waves are emitted; this property is used in radio transmitters to control frequency. Another surprising property of quartz is that if you take two crystals, hold one in each hand under water and hit them together, it produces a flash of light. Amazing! But be careful as they may crack so only use rough material.

Tourmaline also has a rare property in that if a crystal of the gem is heated, an electrical charge is developed along the crystal with opposing poles at each end.

Precious Stones

Sapphire, diamond, ruby and pearl pin. (Photo: WL)

It is important to know some of the characteristics and colours of the different varieties and how they may be 'improved' or faked. The following reference sections on **Precious Stones, Gemstones** and **Organic Gems** give relevant details of the most popular gemstones and a few that are less well known. A short guidance to the identification is also given where appropriate. A couple of inexpensive instruments were detailed earlier to enable you to experiment with identification. The tips given are purely a rough indication of possible fraudulent stones that you may come across. It will certainly not turn you into a gemmologist and it is not intended that you should challenge the dealer or jeweller about his description. However, do trust your new-found knowledge, as well as your instincts: if you mistrust or are unhappy about what a dealer is telling you, then just say, "thank you very much," and walk away.

Although this book includes many helpful photographs, pictures are never as good as the real thing. An excellent idea is to visit museums where gems are on display and educate yourself on what the stones look like in reality. Of course, the quality of the museum specimens is likely to be much higher than anything you should expect to find in shops, but it does get you used to looking at gems. There are some excellent collections to be seen; if you are in London, the Natural History Museum in Kensington has a good display.

DIAMOND

The diamond – the gem that apparently every woman wants, a 'girls best friend', – but what is it exactly? Formed 100-200km under the surface of the earth from 990 million to 3.2 billion years ago, diamond is pure carbon; in fact it is the same thing as pencil lead, just in crystal form. Diamond is the hardest natural material known to man and has many industrial uses, such as to drill for oil. It also used to cut and polish other diamonds.

About 11 to 12 tons of diamond are produced from the earth every year, only about 2 tons of this are of gem quality. To recover this quantity, 200 million tons of ore have to be shifted. The sale and distribution of diamond is strictly controlled by the Diamond Trading Corporation to maintain a stable market. This is done by stocking diamonds at times of overproduction, or when the market is slack, and releasing to dealers when the time is right for the market at an occasion called a 'sight'. This practice has ensured that the price of diamonds has risen consistently.

Dealers, called 'sight holders', have to be registered and are invited to attend a 'sight', at which they are presented with a 'packet' of good and indifferent stones, a mix that they must accept or lose their registration. Consideration is sometimes given to certain sight holders who specialise in particular fields and the packets are 'shaped' to their needs. These 'sights' are held ten times a year. No other gem is handled in this manner. However, the management of the system is under review and will probably change in the near future.

Rough diamonds. (Photo: AH)

The 4 Cs: Colour, Clarity, Cut and Carat

Colour – What colour is a diamond? Blue, yellow, red, pink, brown, green, black? It can be any of these; but I expect that the one in your ring is colourless. Even 'colourless' diamonds are graded into nine different shades, the finest being exceptional white, with cape or tinted colour (a yellowish tinge) as the lowest. These differences are caused by the varying percentages of nitrogen in the stones, the best stones having the least nitrogen content. Most stones you see are 'white' or 'commercial white'. However the colour grading system currently in use is that developed by the Gemmological Institute of America (GIA). This uses letters from D through to Z, where D is the best. (It is unclear why it starts with 'D' rather than 'A'.) Colour is judged by the use of a set of 'master stones' in a special light box.

Clarity – This refers to the 'cleanness' or purity of the stone. Most gemstones contain small impurities, or inclusions; in diamond these are usually small pieces of black carbon, though they can contain other things. Lasers can be used to burn out carbon inclusions from a stone to improve its appearance. Grading is also sub-divided into nine classifications, the top grade being pure or flawless. In fact this means that no inclusions are visible using a ten times magnification lens or loupe, though the stone may well have some inclusions visible under a microscope.

'Pique' means pricked, containing small inclusions usually visible to the naked eye. There have been several versions of colour and purity grading over the years and it varies from country to country, but this one on the right by the GIA is generally accepted at the moment.

As you can see, the distinctions between various degrees of colour and purity are open to a fair amount of expert judgement by the diamond grader and are not something that the layperson can judge for themselves. The tables are given purely as a guide to the meaning of the various terms used when describing stones.

Table 9 Diamond Clarity

Flawless (FL)	Shows no inclusions or blemishes under the 10x loupe
Internally flawless (IF)	Shows no inclusions and only insignificant surface blemishes under the 10x loupe
Very very slightly included(V V S)	Contains minute inclusions that are difficult for an experienced grader to see with a 10x loupe
V V S 1	Contains inclusions that are extremely difficult to see
V V S 2	Contains inclusions that are very difficult to see
Very slightly included (VS)	Shows minor inclusions under a 10x loupe.
V S 1	Contains inclusions that are difficult to see
V S 2	Contains inclusions that are somewhat difficult to see
Slightly included (SI)	Contains noticeable inclusions under 10x loupe
S11	Contains inclusions that are easy to see
S12	Contains inclusions are very easy to see, even with the naked eye.
Imperfect (also known as 'piqued')	Contains obvious inclusions under 10x loupe, which can often be seen easily with the naked eye. They may seriously affect the stone's potential durability or are so numerous they affect the stone's transparency and brilliance.
11	Beauty and durability are somewhat affected.
12	Beauty and durability are seriously affected.
13	Beauty and durability are very seriously affected.

Cut – This, as it sounds, simply describes the way that the stone is cut. For a diamond to display its full beauty and sparkle, the cut has to be correct and follow certain proportions. If a diamond is faceted at the wrong angles, which does sometimes occur to minimise wastage with an awkward piece of rough, it will not give the required dispersion and will affect the fully-internal reflection necessary to allow the diamond to show its full fire. A shallow cut stone is termed a 'fish eye'. Due to the diamond's high refraction and dispersion, all light falling upon it, providing it is correctly cut, is reflected internally; no light should leak out of the back of the stone. If you look full onto the face of a correctly cut diamond, you cannot see through it. Ideal proportions differ, dependent on the refractive indices of the gem, so what is ideal for diamond is not, for instance, ideal for cubic zirconia.

Table 10 gives some of the various cuts that you will come across. These cuts apply equally well to coloured gemstones. In the USA the quality of the cut is often referred to as the 'make'.

This is only a small selection of the great number of cuts that have been used in the past and new styles are still being developed. Recently, new variations of the standard brilliant cut have been marketed; one of these is the 'Eternal Cut' – designed by Gabi Tolkowsky for Asprey & Garrard, it has 81 facets compared to the standard 57.

A Japanese company claims to 'change' the colour of its diamonds by increasing the number of the facets to 86, making a deeper stone in the process. This alters the refraction of light through the gem, accentuating a particular spectral colour.

All faceting of gemstones is carried out in a similar manner, though diamonds are so much harder that they are handled slightly differently. Large diamonds are often cleaved: a hammer and chisel are used to split the gem along natural cleavage planes within the stone. A skilled cutter can take days to decide where he will strike the stone; a wrong choice and the diamond will shatter. Once a large stone has been cleaved, it is handled in the same way as a smaller stone. First it is sawn to a rough

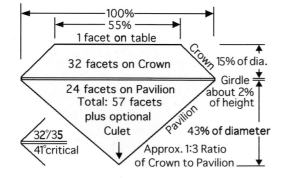

The proportions of an ideal cut diamond brilliant

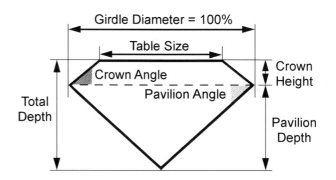

Details of the brilliant cut. (Courtesy of Gem-A)

Table 10 Standard Gemstone Cuts

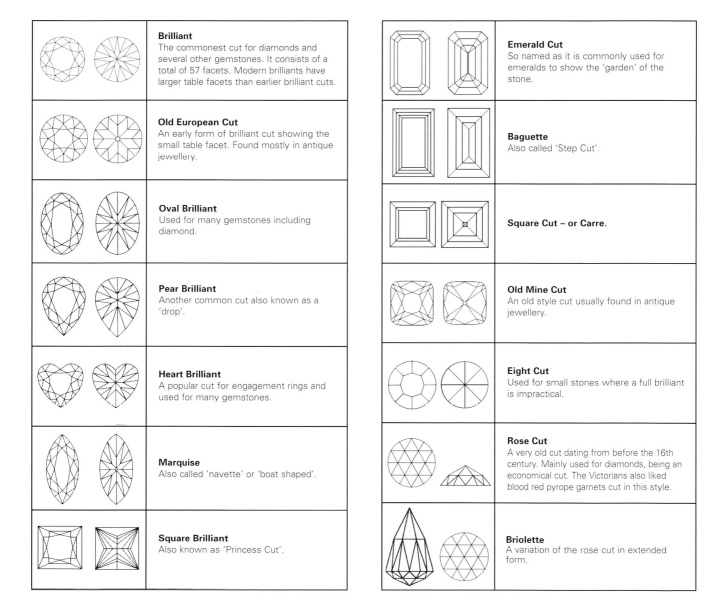

Brilliant
The commonest cut for diamonds and several other gemstones. It consists of a total of 57 facets. Modern brilliants have larger table facets than earlier brilliant cuts.

Old European Cut
An early form of brilliant cut showing the small table facet. Found mostly in antique jewellery.

Oval Brilliant
Used for many gemstones including diamond.

Pear Brilliant
Another common cut also known as a 'drop'.

Heart Brilliant
A popular cut for engagement rings and used for many gemstones.

Marquise
Also called 'navette' or 'boat shaped'.

Square Brilliant
Also known as 'Princess Cut'.

Emerald Cut
So named as it is commonly used for emeralds to show the 'garden' of the stone.

Baguette
Also called 'Step Cut'.

Square Cut – or Carre.

Old Mine Cut
An old style cut usually found in antique jewellery.

Eight Cut
Used for small stones where a full brilliant is impractical.

Rose Cut
A very old cut dating from before the 16th century. Mainly used for diamonds, being an economical cut. The Victorians also liked blood red pyrope garnets cut in this style.

Briolette
A variation of the rose cut in extended form.

shape, then ground into a double cone. Then the stone is passed to the polisher who cuts the facets onto the stone before polishing it. These last two operations are carried out on a lap – a rotating metal disc similar to a potter's wheel – impregnated with diamond powder of decreasing fineness.

In some countries gemstones (though not diamonds) are cut using a jamb peg: a pear-shaped block of wood covered with holes in calculated positions. The 'peg' or dopstick onto which the stone is attached with a special wax, is then inserted in the appropriate hole and the stone fed onto the rotating lap.

Concave faceting is a startling new style of cutting, but availability is limited. Four examples are shown below, but there are many variations.

Mention should also be made here of the cabochon, which, though not used for diamond, is used for many translucent minerals or those showing particular characteristics such as 'star stones'. It was fashionable at one time to cut sapphire in this manner. The cabochon is a dome, sometimes steep sometimes shallow, the name coming from the early French for 'head'.

Example of Jasper cut as a cabochon

Types of cabochon

Simple

Double

Hollow

Examples of concave-cut cubic zirconia. (Photo: CA)

Table 11 Weights of Brilliant Cut Diamonds

Approx. Wt.	Diameter
0.01 ct	1.4 mm
0.05 ct	2.4 mm
0.10 ct	3.0 mm
0.25 ct	4.0 mm
0.50 ct	5.1 mm
0.75 ct	5.8 mm
1.00 ct	6.4 mm
1.50 ct	7.4 mm
2.00 ct	8.1 mm
2.50 ct	8.7 mm
3.00 ct	9.2 mm
3.50 ct	9.8 mm
4.00 ct	10.2 mm

Table 12 Comparative Sizes of Gems

Gemstone	%	Overall Size
Iolite	25.85	
Quartz	24.72	L
Aquamarine	23.58	A
Emerald	23.01	R
Tourmaline	13.35	G
Kunzite	8.81	E
Moissanite	8.52	R
Peridot	5.11	
Tanzanite	4.83	
DIAMOND		**Reference**
Topaz	-0.57	
Spinel	-2.56	S
Hessonite	-3.69	M
Pyrope	-6.53	A
Demantoid	-9.09	L
Ruby	-13.35	L
Sapphire	-13.35	E
Zircon (Normal)	-28.98	R
YAG	-30.11	
Cubic Zirconia	-58.52	

The comparative size of popular gems compared to diamond of equivalent weight e.g. a 1 carat ruby is 13.35% smaller overall than a 1 carat diamond.

Carat – Diamonds are weighed in carats, this is the recognised international standard. (In fact all gems are weighed in carats other than pearls, which come under a different classification and are weighed in grains.) A carat is ⅕ of a gram and is sub-divided into 100 points; there are 5 carats to a gram and 32 grams to a troy ounce.

So why carat? It is believed to have originated from the use of the dried seeds of the 'locust pod' tree (*Ceratonia siliqua*) by early stone dealers to weigh stones due to the seed's weight being so consistent – approximately ⅕ of a gram. The 'metric carat' was finally standardised in various countries in the late 19th and early 20th centuries. The carat weight of stones should not be confused with the karat purity of gold, although the terms are derived from the same source. Originally also called 'carat', karat with a 'k' was introduced in the USA to avoid confusion.

An approximate guide to the weight of a round diamond can be gauged by measuring the diameter of the stone. Table 11 lists weight against diameter in millimetres. It only applies to diamonds cut to near ideal proportions. It does not apply to other gems as their weight varies with their density.

All the 4 Cs should be taken into account when assessing a stone's value and this can vary widely between the same size diamonds. A one-carat stone can be worth from a couple of hundred pounds to many thousands of pounds. Some coloured diamonds, termed 'fancies' by dealers, can rate £30,000 per carat. The rarest coloured diamond is red, followed by green, blue, pink and yellow. There is not a set rate per carat, however: smaller stones rate a low price per carat, the larger the stone the higher carat price.

The real Cullinan 1 (on left) and 2 (on right), shown alongside a one carat diamond for comparison. Shown actual size: Cullinan 1: 58.9mm (2⁵⁄₁₆in) long, 45.4mm (1¾in) wide, 530.2cts. Cullinan 2: 45.4mm (1¾in) maximum diameter, 40.8mm (1⅗in) minimum diameter, 317.4cts. (Photo: AJ)

Famous stones

Perhaps the most famous 'fancy' is the dark blue Hope Diamond, weighing 44.5 carats, which is now on view in the Smithonian Institution in Washington, USA. It has a reputation for being unlucky and a long history. It is believed to have been part of a large blue diamond found in India by a 17th century merchant, Tavernier, who travelled widely and had a great interest in precious stones; it weighed 112 carats in the rough. On Tavernier's return to France he sold it to King Louis XIV, together with some other stones. It was named 'The Blue Diamond of the Crown' and Louis had it cut to improve it, reducing its weight to 67.5 carats.

The diamond was lost during the French Revolution, but in 1830 a similar blue diamond turned up in London, this time only weighing 44.5 carats. It had obviously been recut. Henry Thomas Hope, a banker, bought it for £18,000. Hope's son lost his inherited fortune by investing badly and the gem was sold to the Sultan of Turkey for £80,000. In 1911 it was sold to an American widow who was reported to have lost her only child in an accident, her family broke up and she lost all her money before committing suicide. In 1949, it was bought by Harry Winston, the famous American dealer in New York. He exhibited it at many events world wide, before donating it in 1958 to the Smithsonian, where it now resides, worth several million dollars.

There are many interesting histories associated with large diamonds and some stones can be traced back as far as the 15th century.

The largest diamond found was the Cullinan weighing an astonishing 3,106 carats when discovered in the Premier mine near Pretoria in South Africa in 1905. The Cullinan was cut into 9 major stones and 96 smaller brilliants. Presented to King Edward VII, the largest of the major gems was named the 'Star of Africa' (Cullinan 1; 530.20 carats), which was mounted in the sceptre of the British Crown Jewels, the next largest (Cullinan 2; 317.40 carats) was set into the Imperial State Crown. In fact all of the nine major stones are either in the British Crown Jewels or in the personal possession of the British Royal Family.

The famous 'Koh-i-Noor' emanated from India in the 14th century, passing through many hands before being presented to Queen Victoria in 1850. It now resides in the Queen Mother's crown. It has been recut several times, its current weight is 105.602 carats. Another diamond found in India at about the same time was the 'Great Mogul', weighing a massive 793cts when found; its present whereabouts are unknown.

Diamonds have always been glamorous, not least that given by Richard Burton to Elizabeth Taylor, this famous 'rock' weighed 69.42 carats and was bought for $1 million. Over the past fifteen years some very large diamonds have been sold – the 'Mouawad Splendour' of 101.84 carats sold for $12,800,000, while the 'Star of the Season', of 'D' colour and weighing an enormous 100.10 carats, sold for an equally enormous $16,548,750.

Improvements

I have already mentioned under 'clarity' how lasers can be used to remove unwanted inclusions, but this can leave a minute hole in the table that is sometimes possible to see with the 10x loupe. The vertical drillings may also be seen through the side of the stone unless they have been filled. This treatment is permanent, but does not affect the colour of the stone.

The colour can also be enhanced. This is done by the application of colour coatings to the surface as well as by irradiation and annealing.

Irradiation can produce attractive colours from indifferent stones commonly green. Brown or off-

CZ model of the Taylor-Burton diamond, a 'D' flawless stone, weighing 69.42cts. This stone was famously given by Hollywood actor Richard Burton to Elizabeth Taylor in 1969. A YAG replica was made for everyday wear. Elizabeth Taylor sold the diamond in 1979 for approximately $5m in order to raise funds to build a hospital in Botswana. Shown actual size. (Photo: RH)

CZ model of the famous Hope diamond. Shown actual size. (Photo: RH)

Cullinan Diamond: a model of the rough stone as found in South Africa in 1905 with models of all the major stones cut from it. Centre left is the 'Star of Africa' with Cullinan 2 to its right. (Photo: DTC)

colour diamonds can sometimes be made colourless or an improved colour by heat treatment under high pressure, known as 'HPHT'.

Surface fractures may be filled with glass-like fillers; this treatment is one to avoid – it is not permanent and can be damaged by ultra-sonic cleaning.

Any of these improvements must be declared by the vendor and noted on the sales receipt.

As stated previously, the rarest diamond, in nature, is the red, with only about 50 genuine stones existing. When available on the market they rate hundreds of thousands of pounds per carat. A process has recently been developed capable of producing a red diamond from certain 'naturals'. The girdle of the stones over half a carat are laser engraved to identify their true source. Prices are low compared to a natural red. This leads us into the question of synthetics and simulants.

When is a Diamond not a Diamond?

Like any other precious thing, fakes, forgeries and look-alikes abound.

First, it is important to understand the difference between a simulant and a synthetic. All gemstones are a chemical compound and, as such, have a chemical formula. For instance, quartz (of which citrine and amethyst are a couple of the varieties) is silicon oxide, diamond is carbon, ruby is aluminium oxide and so on. Each one contains certain impurities that cause variations in colour. A simulant is a stone that pretends to be another, but is of different chemical composition. Any stone, natural or otherwise, masquerading as another is called a simulant; common simulants are glass and plastic.

A synthetic is a stone grown in a laboratory and may be a chemical equivalent of the natural stone, or a completely new chemical compound not known in nature. Many of these man-made gems, particularly those with no equivalent in nature, are used to simulate diamond.

The names of the synthetic materials tend to be rather unattractive. This is why, for example, Yttrium aluminium garnet (YAG for short) is marketed as 'Diamonair', 'Geminair', and 'Diamone' and GGG (Gadolinium gallium garnet) is marketed as 'Galliant' to name but two of many. (Originally both GGG and YAG were called 'Diamonique', but this is now the trademark name for cubic zirconia owned by QVC, the TV shopping company.)

All these stones are very attractive. A few were first developed for the laser industry and found their way into the jewellery market. Their main drawback is their hardness, or lack of it. They are much, much softer than diamond and, remember, it is a diamond's hardness that gives the sharp edges to the facets, which last and last; as the song says: "Diamonds are Forever". After several years, wear on the softer synthetic stones will round off these edges.

The emergence of cubic zirconia (CZ) in the mid-seventies made an enormous and serious impact on the trade. Its characteristics are very close to that of diamond, except that it is heavier, size for size. However, the extra weight is of little consequence when set in jewellery, as most are. Many jewellers were conned by these new synthetic stones until the introduction of economically priced test instruments. CZ has now taken its place in the shops as an accepted 'jewel' and is available in a variety of colours, the yellow being a very convincing simulant of yellow diamond. Though it has been reported that CZ has a tendency to take on a grey tone after prolonged exposure to daylight.

A new problem has occurred recently and that is the introduction of synthetic 'Moissanite' on to the market. Apart from being doubly refractive, which diamond is not, it is very hard, comparable to ruby or sapphire, and is far more convincing than cubic zirconia. However 'Moissanite' does not come in colours better than 'J' so may appear slightly yellowish compared to a good coloured diamond. Diamonds are now usually tested using a thermal conductivity measuring device, which will identify all simulants except moissanite. To detect moissanite, a special moissanite tester must be used; ensure that the tester being used to prove a diamond to you is this special tester.

Moissanite was initially discovered accidentally by Professor Moisson in the late 1890s when he was trying to make diamond, but has only recently been rediscovered.

I should make it clear that these simulants are not produced with the intention of fooling anybody, but as an inexpensive alternative to the real thing, although Moissanite is still at a high price, several times that of CZ and YAG. This price is now being challenged by the rapidly increasing production of synthetic diamonds. The danger comes when the unscrupulous purchase them with the direct intention of defrauding the unsuspecting buyer.

Genuine gemstones, such as rock crystal, white sapphire, white topaz and zircon, are also sometimes offered as diamonds.

Even diamond crystals have been faked. Some diamond crystals are like a double pyramid called an octahedron and these have been copied in glass; quite convincing for the unaware, but obvious to the expert.

Mounted stones can also be suspect. Always view enclosed settings where the girdle cannot be seen with caution. Diamonds as well as many other gems can be made as 'doublets'. This is where a slice of genuine stone is fused to a body of a cheaper material, such as glass or quartz to form a table, which to cursory inspection could give the impression that the whole stone is diamond. This fools testers like reflectometers.

A rare diamond forgery is the 'piggy-back' designed to give the appearance of a large stone when, in fact, it consists of two separate pieces.

Diamonds can now be grown in the laboratory. Although experiments began in the nineteenth century,

Examples of composite stones

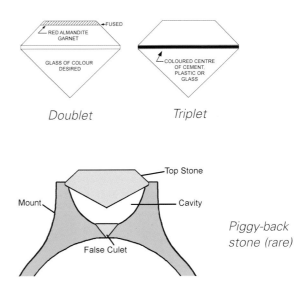

Doublet   *Triplet*

Piggy-back stone (rare)

successful manufacture only began in the 1950s and viable commercial processes have only been achieved within the last twenty years. The main suppliers are Chatham Created Gems, who produce 500 carats of synthetic diamond rough of all colours a month. Manufactured in China under licence, each of their stones over 50 points or half a carat is engraved on the girdle to identify them.

Gemesis in the USA also produces yellow diamonds, similarly engraved. Both companies use the HPHT method of growth. It is believed, however, that there are many other companies of varying size also producing synthetic diamonds. As yet, white stones are more expensive to produce than coloured ones, so less competitive with the natural gems. Consequently, most 'created' diamonds on the market are coloured. This situation will continue to grow so, if you are buying

Chatham-created diamonds. (Photo: Chatham)

large diamonds for investment, be sure to obtain a certification from a recognised test laboratory.

At the moment, the cost of the equipment to manufacture 'laboratory diamonds' is very high but new methods are reducing these costs. It is only a matter of time before synthetic diamonds are as commonplace as synthetic rubies and emeralds. However the effect on the diamond market is not expected to be any more severe than that has been caused by other synthetic gems. The gemmological laboratories, such as the Gem Testing Laboratory of Great Britain, GIA and particularly De Beers are keeping ahead of these developments and will continue to protect the trade against unscrupulous traders, producing sophisticated test instruments to identify these synthetics.

There are many more synthetic gems produced, whose often names usually beginning with 'dia-', though this is illegal, a fact that is generally ignored. It should also be remembered that when 'diamond' is prefixed

Doubling of back facets in moissanite. (Photo: AH)

with a name i.e. 'Saudi Diamond' or 'Bristol Diamond' these are not actually diamond, but generally quartz.

One new development in the sale of cubic zirconia is Czarite, produced by the famous crystal producers Swarovski. They claim to cut their CZ at its ideal proportions giving it maximum brilliance. A 'Starscope' is provided with the stone so that you can view the pavilion of the gem through it and see the 'star' so formed. A real diamond will not show this 'star' because it is cut to its own ideal proportion, which are different to CZ.

All this leaves a question in your mind – do you want a real diamond that took millions of year to develop in the earth and laboriously mined, or one that is churned out by machine in the factory?

Table 13 Some Names Used for Diamond Simulants

Trade Name	Synthetic Stone
Czarite	CZ
Diagem	ST
Diamante	CZ
Diamone	YAG
Diamonaire	YAG
Diamonite	CZ
Diamonique	YAG, CZ
Diamond Essence	CZ
Diamonte	YAG
Fabulite	ST
Geminair	YAG
Phianite	CZ
Regulaire	YAG

CZ = (Cubic Zirconia)
ST = (Strontium Titanate)
YAG = (Yttrium Aluminium Garnet)

Just as a parting thought on diamond - a company in the USA is offering to add some of the ashes of your dear departed into a synthetic yellow diamond made to order. The stones, made in a range of sizes, run into thousands of pounds depending on carat size.

Telling the difference

How can the layperson distinguish a real diamond from the many simulants and synthetics? Here are a few tips:

1. Place the stone, preferably unmounted, table up on a piece of printed-paper. If you can see the print through the table, it is not a diamond. This only works with a well-cut modern round brilliant but not with old cut stones and fancy cuts. Beware, some less well-cut CZ and moissanite stones will pass this test.

2. Ensure that the stone is clean. Take a black felt tip pen and draw a line across the table of the diamond. If the line breaks up, i.e. is not continuous, the stone is unlikely to be a genuine diamond. This is because diamonds have an affinity for grease; a property used for sorting them at the mines: a greased conveyor belt is used so that the diamonds stick to it and the rubbish does not. This form of sorting is now being replaced by X-ray.

3. Look at the facets through the 10x loupe, if they are rounded and not sharp or show signs of chipping the stone is probably not genuine. This chipping occurs particularly with zircons so is a good method of identification. However if the diamond is old it may show signs of chipping.

4. Moissanite and zircon are doubly refractive and careful study of the stone through the kite facets will show a doubled image of the opposite facet edges. Diamond, of course is singly refractive.

5. Cubic Zirconia is heavier, size for size, than diamond

6. Cubic Zirconia is often identified with the use of a thermal conductivity tester. As this instrument is expensive, a simple (and cheap) way to test a diamond is to hold the stone in tongs and touch it with the tip of your tongue. Diamond will feel much colder than simulants (except Moissanite). Another way is to breathe on the face of the stone; the condensation will clear more rapidly on the diamond.

7. Looking at the depth of colour under the loupe may identify irradiated diamonds, commonly green although other colours may be seen. Irradiation is a surface enhancement, so the shallower parts of the stone i.e near the girdle may appear darker.

6. Check for engraved girdles on larger stones.

Alan Hodgkinson, the President of the Scottish Branch of Gem-A, developed a startling method of identifying diamond from any other colourless stone in the mid-seventies called 'Visual Optics'; with a little practice, it is within the grasp of a keen layperson.

You require a darkened room and a single point of light positioned at a distance from your seat; a torch or even a candle will do. Holding the crown or table facet of the suspect diamond as close to your eye as possible (touching your eyelashes) and look at the light, closing your eye to a narrow slit, so that all you can see is the

Thermal conductivity tester. (Photo: KW)

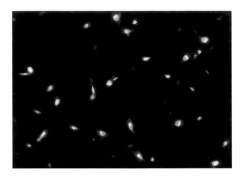

Diamond. (Photo: AH)

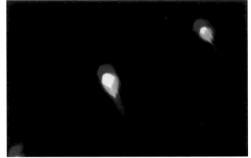

Moissanite. (Photo: AH)

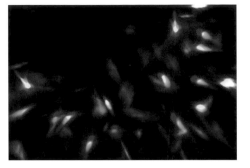

Cubic Zirconia. (Photo: AH)

light coming through the stone. Slowly move your eye around the stone until you see an image. This will require a bit of practice but it is worth persevering.

The random pattern of tiny sharp images in diamond is entirely diagnostic. No other gemstone shows this. So if this is what you see, you have a diamond. Any other pattern tells you it is not diamond. The larger blurred flakes in synthetic Moissanite give it away immediately. The singly refractive CZ is again so different to diamond that identification is simple.

In the case of diamond and synthetic moissanite the pattern is formed by secondary reflections due to the high refraction, but the patterns seen in CZ are primary reflections from the pavilion facets due to its lower R.I.

No other gem will give you the same pattern as diamond (except synthetic diamond). The technique also works with set stones, unless they have a closed back. Larger stones are easier to handle but, with practice, quite small stones may be identified using this method.

The 'Hodgkinson Technique' works with all transparent gemstones, coloured or not, but for the purposes of this book we will only consider its use with identifying diamonds.

Just one point of interest before we leave diamonds, some diamonds fluoresce under ultra-violet light (sometimes used in discos); usually blue or yellow but not all, so don't worry if one stone in your ring fluoresces and the others don't, it doesn't matter.

Visual optics. (Photo: JP)
This picture is indicative only, in reality the light source must be further away from the viewer – at least 10ft. A penlight is ideal, the candle is a last resort

Emerald

Emerald is a member of the Beryl family, which consists of Beryl (commonly green) itself, Aquamarine (blue), Morganite (pink), Heliodor (yellow) and Goshenite (colourless). Only green Beryl containing chromium is classed as emerald, because it is this impurity that gives the gem its beautiful colour.

Emerald is rarely free of inclusions and these are sometimes referred to as the 'garden' of the stone. Colour is all-important in emerald, inclusions are secondary. Look through the table of one with a magnifying glass and explore, it can be a wonderland. A perfect emerald can outrank a diamond in value.

Fractures are also common, which raises the controversial subject of filling. Filling has been used for very many years and consists of glass or resins. Oils are often used to improve the appearance. Arguments have been going on in the trade as to whether filling or oiling should be declared. The general feeling is no, but agents to improve the colour must be stated.

Emeralds must be handled with care: any oil used to improve the appearance will be removed by overheating or detergents, so be careful.

Ultrasonic cleaners should also be avoided, as they can cause the stone to shatter, so specify this to your jeweller should you take your jewellery in for cleaning or repair. A reputable jeweller will already be aware of this. Even repairs to a ring where heat is required can damage any filling the stone has received and weaken it.

The current sources of emerald are Colombia, Brazil, Russia, Australia, South Africa, India plus a few minor sources. Recently, finds of gem quality have been made in Canada. A rare form of emerald, the Trapiche (tra-PEE-chee), is only found in Colombia. Its name comes from the spoked cog-wheel used to grind sugarcane, as the stone displays a spoke-like pattern, which gives a six-pointed star effect.

Large emeralds are very rare, particularly those of good colour. One of the biggest found in the early

A pear-shaped cabochon-cut Canadian emerald (2.10cts) enlarged to show 'garden'. (Photo: TNG)

nineteenth century in Colombia was the 'Devonshire', which weighed in at 1383.95 carats uncut.

Fakes and frauds

Because emerald is such a valuable stone simulants abound. The value and popularity can be judged by the enormous trade in smuggled stones costing governments, such as that of Brazil, hundreds of millions of pounds a year.

Common simulants are doublets and triplets as shown earlier; often referred to as 'Soude' emeralds.

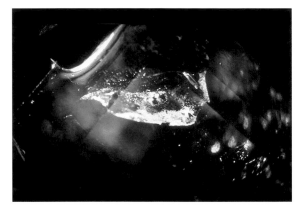

Fracture-filled stone. (Photo: RH)

An unusually clear emerald from the Mouzo mine in Colombia (0.37cts enlarged). (Photo: AJ)

Colombian emerald showing typical 'garden'. (Photo: RH)

The triplets are two pieces of quartz with a green gelatine layer sandwiched between, although other materials may be used to create the same effect. The painting of the backs of natural pale emeralds has also been tried.

Several companies produce synthetic emerald legitimately, the best known being the American company Chatham. (Gilson, which was one of the forerunners of synthetic emerald, was taken over by Chatham in the late 1990s). Originally synthesised in the early 20th century, it was only with the emergence of Gilson and Chatham in the 1930s that synthetic emeralds began to take their place as an accepted alternative to the natural gem in the jewellery trade.

Chemically identical to the natural stone and virtually undetectable by the layperson, synthetic emeralds sell at about a tenth of the price of the real stones. Russia and Japan also produce synthetics.

Cartier brooch. Carved emeralds, amethysts and diamonds c.1940. (Photo: WL)

A display of emeralds from the new source in the Yukon, (enlarged). Generally of small size, under 0.5cts. (Photo: TNG)

As the availability of natural emerald from the classic source of Colombia fluctuates due to mines being closed down on a regular basis caused by criminal activity, synthetics will always be there to satisfy demand for one of the most popular of gems.

The Chelsea Filter was initially developed to identify the numerous simulants from the real emerald stones, which show red under the filter due to the chromium present. However, the Gilson & Chatham synthetics also show red under the filter, but to differing degrees. Other green simulants mostly do show green under the Chelsea Filter except demantoid garnet and zircon, which show pinkish. Chrome tourmaline a beautiful green gem will also show red under the filter. Yet another snag is that some emeralds contain iron and so do not show red at all under the filter. I am afraid you must rely on a gemmologist to confirm the identity.

Emeralds have always been a popular gem to synthesise and simulate so it is still possible to find early examples of these. Lechleitner synthetics consisted of a piece of faceted common beryl with a thin coating of synthetic emerald 'grown' over to give the appearance of a solid stone. This would give all the characteristics of a natural stone. These appeared in the 1960s.

Ruby. (Photo: RH)

Star Ruby.
(Photo: RH)

Ruby

Ruby and Sapphire are chemically very similar, both are corundum, only colour differentiates them due to chromium in ruby and titanium in sapphire. The best ruby comes from Myanmar (formerly Burma) and the best colour is 'pigeon blood', but stones of this quality are rare and very expensive. Thailand, Tanzania and Madagascar (formerly the Malagasy Republic) also produce stones but rarely of the quality of the Myanmar stones. Sri Lanka, which has the greatest variety of gemstones, also provides rubies, most of which are pale, but occasionally intense reds are discovered. Pale red colours are actually classified as pink sapphire. New sources of stones are being discovered with regularity. Rubies are 'the' investment stone. Large crystals over five carats are very rare and a lot is lost in cutting, due to colour variations.

Rubies often contain inclusions called 'silk', caused by needle-like crystals of rutile. The inclusions sometimes form in such a way as to produce what is known as a 'star ruby'. These are cut *en cabochon* orientated to display the star. They are highly prized and expensive.

Of course these can also be forged by engraving lines on the base of the cabochon and covering with a piece of reflective material or synthesised in the laboratory. Natural star stones rarely show the stars as bright and clear as the 'forgeries'.

Consequently synthetic ruby abounds, tons being pro-duced every year. Chatham from the USA also produces high-quality stones that are extremely difficult to detect without laboratory help. A particularly good synthetic ruby has been produced in Mexico under the name of 'Ramaura Rubies' created by the J.O. Crystal Company. A special fluorescent dopant is added to enable identification by the gemmologist.

The synthetic stones can be of such high quality that you may not mind whether you have a real ruby or not – after all, if you don't know whether the gem in your ring is real or synthetic, neither will your friends. The thing to avoid is paying the price of real for synthetic. If, however, you decide that only the real thing will do, then the only answer is to go to a reputable supplier. Inclusions and colour banding usually identify natural stones from synthetic, but of course this is the job of a qualified gemmologist. Glass filling of fractures is becoming more common, so if a stone is being bought as an investment, then it is imperative to have it checked at a laboratory before purchase.

Other red-coloured natural gems are sometimes confused with ruby, such as spinels and red garnets, though both of these are singly refractive and not doubly refractive as is ruby.

Ruby has been misidentified for hundreds of years. The 170 ct. Black Prince's 'ruby' originally set in the helmet of King Henry V and worn at the battle of Agincourt is, in fact, a spinel; it is now set in the Imperial State Crown.

Rubies, diamonds, platinum and gold, c.1900. (Photo: WL)

Sapphire

Much of what has been said about ruby applies just as well to sapphire, except of course that the usually accepted colour is blue. The best colours are the rare Kashmir Blue from India and Cornflower Blue, but sapphires are also found in a range of other hues: pink, orange, yellow, green and mauve, in fact any corundum that is not a strong red or blue is termed 'fancy sapphire'.

Sapphire is found in many places in the world, Australia (usually darker shades), Sri Lanka, Myanmar (Burma), Africa, Thailand, Canada and the USA. Strangely enough they have also been discovered in Scotland. A colour change variety is found in Sri Lanka and East Africa.

Synthetics abound; synthetic corundum is produced in a wide range of colours to simulate many gemstones. Chatham synthesises blue, pink, green, purple and yellow sapphire. The orange or 'padparadsha' sapphire is perhaps the most valuable gemstone when in good colour; the best have a pinkish tinge; a particularly striking stone and highly collected, it has also been synthesised by Chatham and Seiko of Japan. Yellow sapphire is also popular and difficult to identify. The majority, including the golden sapphire, are beryllium treated, so best avoided. There is also a natural colourless variety, of relatively low value that has been used as a diamond simulant. Surprisingly, this has also been synthesised and is commonly used for watch-glasses.

Star sapphires are also produced and the remarks made about star rubies apply equally to sapphire. Colours include blue, pink, violet and brown, the near black variety is particularly striking. As with rubies, fakes also occur of star sapphires.

To distinguish between synthetic and natural sapphire is not easy without instruments, however it may be possible with a loupe to see the growth lines – usually curved in the synthetic stones, straight in the natural stone.

Colour zoning occurs in both natural and synthetic. Natural sapphire is strongly dichroic showing pale greenish-blue and dark blue. Chatham synthetics show violet blue and greenish-blue.

Carved sapphire surrounded by diamonds, c.1900.
(Photo: WL)

Some of the many colours of sapphire. (Photo: RH)

Ceylon sapphires, rubies and ruby beads. (Photo: WL)

Blue synthetic spinel and cobalt glass show shades of red to pink under the Chelsea filter, whereas sapphire shows a dirty green. Transparent blue stones that show red, orange or pink under the filter must be suspect. However, some Sri Lankan sapphires may show red due to a trace of chromium.

The darker blue Tanzanite may be mistaken for sapphire but the strong pleochroism (three colours) should indicate the difference. Unfortunately heat treatment of the stones can dull this effect.

Blue tourmaline and blue zircon (also heat treated) are also used as simulants. The former shows dichroism of light blue and dark blue whereas zircon is identified by its strong 'fire'.

The Gemstones

This section describes most of the gemstones to be found in the high street jewellers or offered on television shopping channels or over the internet. Some will only be available from specialist dealers. (A separate section deals with minor stones on page 94).

ANDALUSITE

An attractive gemstone, the andalusite takes its name from Andalusia in Spain, where it was first discovered. It has since also been found in Sri Lanka and Brazil.

Andalusite has a hardness of 7½ on the Mohs scale, so is very suitable for a ringstone. It is extremely pleochroic: it shows different colours in different directions – yellow, green and red. If you are after something distinctive, this stone will fit the bill.

Similar shades of tourmaline are sometimes passed off as andalusite, but they lack the pleochroism

Chiastolite, an impure opaque variety of andalusite, is found in the Pyrenees. The carboniferous inclusions form a cross, hence its other name: 'Cross Stone'. It also occurs in several other locations around the world.

Andalusite has two associated gems, termed polymorphs: **Sillimanite** and **Kyanite**, which are occasionally cut and used in jewellery. Although hard, they are somewhat fragile, so the choice of mount is important.

Andalusite, note the pleochroism. (Photo: MM)

Sillimanite occurs in many countries. Rarely transparent, suitable stones for mounting are an attractive pale or violet blue.

Kyanite occurs in blade-like crystals in colours approaching the blue of sapphire. The size of cut gems is limited due to the crystal form, which has the very unusual property of having two hardnesses, 7 in one direction and 4 in the other, causing problems when faceting.

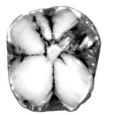

Chiastolite.
(Photo: KW)

Chiastolite beads. (Photo: MM)

Kyanite crystal. (Photo: KW)

Aquamarine.
(Photo: Sotheby's)

AQUAMARINE

A member of the Beryl family, along with emerald, but of a beautiful sea blue colour. Stones are quite often greenish when found but are heat treated to reduce any green cast. This is a very popular gem, more valuable in the larger sizes as small stones usually lack the intensity of colour. It is not subject to the included nature of emerald and quite often found in large water-clear crystals. It is found mainly in Brazil, Russia, Africa and the USA.

Synthetics are not particularly common, but simulants are produced in synthetic corundum, garnet-topped doublets and glass. Blue synthetic spinels also pass themselves off as aquamarine but, like sapphire, aquamarines show dirty green under the Chelsea filter not the pinkish-red of synthetic spinel. Blue topaz can also be mistaken for this gem, the only simple guide is that topaz has a very high polish and a slippery feel compared to aquamarine.

Top right. Fabergé aquamarine and diamond, c.1900 (Photo: WL)

Right. Detail of tiara by Fouquet, aquamarine, pearl and diamond, 1908. (Photo: WL)

BENITOITE

Discovered in America in 1907, this gem was originally thought to be sapphire due to its beautiful blue colour, but was later found to be an entirely new variety.

It has a hardness of 6½ on the Mohs scale, shows excellent fire, and is strongly dichroic (blue and colourless). Its dichroism differentiates it from sapphire, as the latter does not have a colourless ray. Benitoite is rare as it is only found in one part of the USA. It is a very valuable and expensive gem and needs care in its handling. It is the official state stone of California.

Benitoite also occurs in a pink variety.

Benitoite. (Photo: NHM)

BERYL

We have already discussed some of the beryllium gems, namely emerald and aquamarine, but we should also mention the lesser-known members of the same family.

Green Beryl, without the chromium that makes it emerald, is common and, because of its colour, is not particularly attractive. However, it is used in doublets and triplets to simulate emerald.

Heliodor or 'golden beryl' pendant. (Photo: Christie's)

Heliodor or **yellow beryls**, with shades varying from pale to rich gold, are found in the same locations as aquamarine. As with the latter it is often free of inclusions.

Morganite is a pink variety named after the American banker and philanthropist Henry Pierpoint Morgan. It comes in shades of rose and peach as well as pink. Morganite is mainly translucent; cat's-eye varieties have been found. It is generally pale, though dark shades from Madagascar (formerly the Malagasy Republic) and Afghanistan may show dichroism. Its other main source is the USA. Synthetic transparent pink beryls are now grown in Russia.

Red Beryl or **Bixbite** in good gem quality is very rare and, as such, remains a collector's item. It is sometimes misleadingly referred to as 'red emerald'. A deeper blue of beryl darker than aquamarine has been recently discovered in Canada. A colourless variety (Goshenite) is also found.

Morganite.
(Photo: KW)

CHAROITE

Discovered in Eastern Siberia near the River Chara in 1978, charoite is an opaque mineral of a very attractive violet colour with minor inclusions of other minerals. It has a hardness of 5 to 6 on the Mohs scale and takes a good polish, rendering it suitable for use in jewellery and to make carved boxes and ornaments.

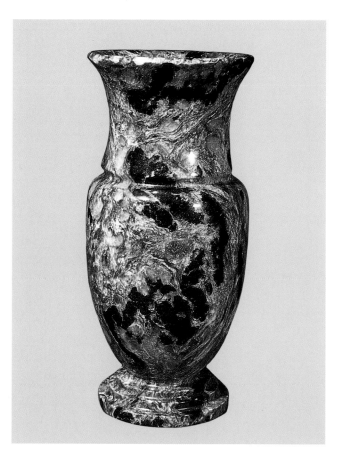

Charoite vase. (Photo: ΛJ)

CHRYSOBERYL

Chrysoberyl is renowned for two famous types of gemstone – cat's-eye and alexandrite.

Alexandrite: seen (left) in daylight and (right) under a tungsten lamp. (Photo: MM)

Alexandrite is a highly prized gemstone, mainly because of its unusual feature of changing colour from grass green when viewed in daylight to rich red when seen in artificial light.

It was originally discovered in the Ural mountains in 1830. As the strongest colours are red and green, the colours of Imperialist Russia, the stone was named after Czar Alexander II, who came of age on the day it was discovered. It has subsequently been found in Sri Lanka, Myanmar (Burma), Brazil, Madagascar (Malagasy Republic) and Zambia. However, the Russian stones are still the most highly prized.

With a hardness of 7.5 on the Mohs scale it makes an excellent

Chrysoberyl. (Photo: ʀH)

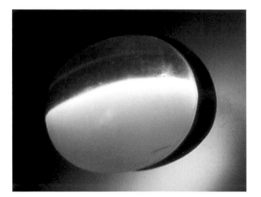

Chrysoberyl cats-eye. (Photo: RH)

a layer of colour gelatine, also give a colour change. These should be treated as any other doublet.

Remember, when buying alexandrite it must show a distinct colour change to be of value. The red and green of the Russian stones are rare, but good stones from Brazil show pinkish red and bluish green and are highly collected. Clarity is not as important as colour. A blue-green variety that fails to show the colour change is being offered. Chatham of the USA produces a synthetic with a good colour change. Some synthetic alexandrite, apparently from Russia, has been offered at recent gem-shows as genuine, but it is not.

Cat's-eye is a chatoyant variety of Chrysoberyl correctly called **Cymophane**. It is usually found in shades of green or yellow; the cat's-eye effect is due to microscopic needles or canals within the crystal. These gems are cabochon cut to show the chatoyance to its full advantage, a sharp bright band across the stone. Good examples are very expensive.

Chrysoberyl also occurs as plain yellow and brown stones without cat's-eye and can be extremely attractive. Quartz cat's-eyes are sometimes sold as Chrysoberyl.

ring stone. It is, however, one of the more expensive gemstones, worth from about £900 per carat up.

Due to its high value it has been the subject of simulants: both synthetic corundum and synthetic spinel are produced in colour change copies, though neither show the strong green and red of the genuine stone. Certain doublets, consisting of rock crystal sandwiching

CHRYSOCOLLA

Chrysocolla is a copper mineral composed of a mix of various microscopic crystals found in a variety of colours. By itself it is too soft (H2-4) to be used, but it is found impregnating quartz or opal. In these cases the green and greenish-blue varieties, cut *en cabochon*, are very attractive. It is found in the USA, Congo, Russia, Chile and Australia. It is also occasionally found in Cornwall.

Similar to chrysocolla, but an even more varied mix of copper minerals, 'Eilat Stone' was supposedly found in the mines of King Solomon. It is blue to green in colour and has been compared to malachite. It is a popular souvenir for tourists. It is Israel's national stone.

Chrysocolla. (Photo: MM)

DANBURITE

Named after Danbury, Connecticut USA where it was discovered, gem-quality danburite was actually first found in Myanmar (Burma). It has since been discovered in Madagascar (Malagasy Republic) and Mexico.

It is a very attractive, if unusual, gem in wine, yellow, pink and colourless varieties. It rates a 7 on the Mohs Scale thereby qualifying as an acceptable jewellery stone. Danburite, however, does not have a very strong fire.

There are no known synthetics as yet. It is heat sensitive, so care is required when repairing jewellery set with them.

A dark orange variety has been reported from Russia but is a rarity.

Danburite. (Photo: AJ)

Diaspore.
(Photo: ATG/Stephen Kotlowski)

DIASPORE

Only recently introduced onto the market, diaspore (pronounced 'die-a-spore' or 'dee-ass-pra') is a colour-change stone similar to a medium-quality alexandrite. Its change from greenish-brown in daylight to pinkish bronze in tungsten light cannot compare with Russian alexandrite but still makes it an interesting gem. It has also been found in a champagne colour, similar to a pale citrine, and brown. Although known in its mineral form for some years, it was not discovered in facetable quality until 1977 in Turkey.

The major source for this gem is still Turkey, but it is likely that material suitable for faceting will be found in other parts of the world. The mineral is found in the USA, South Africa and Norway.

Care should be taken in wearing diaspore as it has a strong cleavage and may chip if knocked.

DUMORTIERITE

Named after a French palaeontologist, Eugene Dumortier, it is sometimes called the 'blue denim stone' because of its deep blue to violet blue colouring. Rarely found as crystals, it is generally used in cabochon form in jewellery or cut into beads, eggs or spheres. It is relatively hard averaging 7 on the Mohs scale. It may be mistaken for lapis lazuli or sodalite, though the latter contains more white areas and is less dense. Dumortierite has a fibrous nature where lapis or lazulite have not. It is used in China as a simulant of lapis lazuli.

Dumortierite in quartz.
(Photo: KW)

It also occurs in a cat's eye variety and blue crystals are sometimes included in massive quartz.

It is said that when worn it gives a clear-headed approach to life and improves organising abilities.

Dumortierite is found in France, several States of America, Brazil, Siberia, India and Madagascar (Malagasy Republic).

FELDSPARS

The feldspar group consists of about 20 members, found in abundance on Earth, though few produce gem material. The forms of interest to us are amazonite, labradorite, moonstone, orthoclase and sunstone.

Amazonite. (Photo: KW)

Amazonite is a blue-green opaque variety, mainly sourced from India and Brazil.

Labradorite from Madagascar. (Photo: KW)

Labradorite is found in Labrador, but not exclusively: Finland is a well-known locality where it is sometimes referred to as 'Spectrolite'.

It has a lovely display of interference colours of blues, greens, yellows, gold, reds and purples shining out of the grey mineral bed. There are other varieties of this stone, though they are not common.

Normally opaque, transparent material has been found in the Congo and in Oregon, USA and cut gems produced.

Moonstone (Photo: AJ)

Moonstone is the most popular feldspar, with its beautiful adularescence, the blue schiller that drifts over an clear opalescent sea. A very romantic stone.

The effect is caused by interference of light within the stone. It is not as hard as other gemstones, about 6 on the Mohs Scale, and with a relatively low density.

It is found in Sri Lanka, India, Madagascar (Malagasy Republic), Myanmar (Burma), Tanzania and the USA.

Simulants are few and should not be confused. Moonstone has identifying inclusions, sometimes called 'caterpillars', these stress cracks are diagnostic, though not all stones have them.

The best is found in Sri Lanka where it is sometimes referred to as the National Stone. Moonstone may also be found in India, Madagascar (Malagasy Republic), Myanmar (Burma), Tanzania and the USA. Rainbow moonstone,

mostly from India, shows the same adularescence, but with a rainbow play of colour. Other varieties exhibit different background colours.

Simulants are few though some glass fakes are convincing except that they are singly refractive, whereas moonstone is doubly refractive.

Orthoclase, also called 'Noble Orthoclase' is sometimes found as transparent golden yellow crystals with a vitreous lustre. They are rare and only cut for collectors. They are of low value.

Sunstone is similar to labradorite except the colours displayed are primarily orange and red. It may sometimes be translucent.

Main sources are Norway, Russia, India, Canada and the USA.

Rainbow moonstone. (Photo: MM)

Sunstone. (Photo: MM)

Blue John. (Photo: KW)

Natural fluorspar octahedron. (Photo: RH)

FLUORSPAR/FLUORITE

Though fluorspar is not generally looked upon as a gemstone because of its relative softness (it rates only 4 on the Mohs Scale), with care, it may be used decoratively.

A very English mineral, it is found in Cornwall and Derbyshire. Its main claim to fame is the unique variety 'Blue John', which is found only in Derbyshire. Although supplies are now limited it was very popular in Victorian times, providing beautiful carved ornaments. Although called 'blue' it has more of a purple colour banding together with browns and yellows. The crystal structure of fluorite shows as chevron layers within a massive material. The Blue John Caverns are a popular tourist venue even today. Classic pieces of Blue John command high prices and many fine examples are to be found in museums. It is notoriously difficult to work and has to be impregnated with resin before carving to stop it splitting across the strong cleavage planes.

Blue John. (Photo: JH)

Blue John Chalice. (Photo: AJ)

It is possible to find excellent examples of cubic crystals of fluorspar in Derbyshire and Cornwall.

Emerald green fluorspar is found in West Africa and has been sold as 'South African Emerald'. It is found in its other colours of yellow, pink, purple and colourless in several parts of the world.

Fluorspar has important industrial uses as flux in the production of steel and in the optical industry as specialist lenses.

A selection of gem fluorspar in facetable quality has recently been discovered in Mozambique. Green, bronze, pink and bi-coloured stones have been cut. They are very attractive, but suitable only for the collector's display cabinet, not for use in jewellery.

A few of the garnet family including hessonite and tsavorite.
(Photo: AJ)

GARNET

This gemstone is a complex range consisting of two basic series, so we will not trouble to go into the chemistry.

Let us just take the colours of the different garnets that you are likely to come across.

Rhodolite garnet.
(Photo: RH)

Dark red – often called 'carbuncles' and much loved by the Victorians, these may be **pyrope**, **almandine** or **rhodolite**. They are found in many parts of the world: Sri Lanka, Central Europe, North and South America, Australia and India.

Dark red garnet may be mistaken for ruby though garnet shows a duller red under the Chelsea Filter than natural or synthetic ruby. Star varieties are also found.

Green – these may be **demantoid** or **tsavorite**. The beautiful demantoid has a greater fire than diamond, but is only 6½ on the Mohs scale of hardness. It is a variety of andradite and has an adamantine lustre like diamond. Demantoid is found in the Urals and Zimbabwe.

Tsavorite garnet.
(Photo: RH)

Yellowish-orange to *brownish-red* – these may be **hessonite** (sometimes called 'Cinnamon Stone') or **spessartine**, found mainly in Sri-Lanka, Brazil and the U.S.A.

Malayan garnet.
(Photo: RH)

Rope of garnets. (Photo: KW)

Giuliano. Garnet and pearl, c.1890.
(Photo: WL)

Tsavorite, discovered in 1967, at its best is bright green, but may be bluish, greyish or pink.

It has been found in Kenya, New Zealand, Pakistan and Myanmar (Burma).

Massive green grossular garnet may be confused with jade and is sometimes called 'Transvaal Jade'.

Colour change – a colour change garnet, similar to alexandrite, is found in Madagascar (Malagasy Republic). The change is from green or lavender to red.

Colourless – these transparent colourless 'garnets' such as YAG, GAG etc, mentioned under diamonds, as simulants are not strictly speaking true garnets as they do not contain silica.

Demantoid garnet. (Photo: MM)

Opal, diamond and demantoid garnets, c.1890. (Photo: WL)

Paste earrings. (Photo: JH)

Bracelet with large oval navelle-cut 'sapphire' crystals, typical of the Austro-Hungarian style. Fine costume jewellery is highly collectible today for its historic significance and creative value. Fine pieces are being sought after by museums worldwide.

(Image from *Vintage Costume Jewellery*

© 2006 Carole Tanenbaum

© 2006 The Antique Collectors' Club)

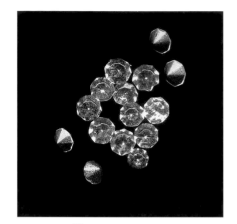

Chatons. (Photo: KW)

GLASS & PASTE

You may consider it strange to include glass here under gems, but it is the most commonly used simulant for most of the gems. Two types of glass are used as simulants, Crown Glass and Flint Glass.

Crown glass is the same material used in the manufacture of bottles and windows. It is generally moulded and used for the cheapest types of jewellery.

Flint glass, however, is much more important for the gemmologist as it produces some very convincing fakes. Lead oxide is used in its manufacture, often supplemented with thallium compounds to increase its brilliance. The best 'gems' are cut and faceted just like conventional stones; cheaper ones are moulded but finished and polished on a lap.

To increase the reflection and fire of some glass 'gems' they are backed with foil or mirrored then painted with gold lacquer, these are called 'chatons'.

These glass imitations come in all colours to imitate very many gemstones. The hardness of glass varies but is usually between 5 and 7; it has a specific gravity between 2.00 and 4.20 depending on the lead content. The easiest method of identification is to look for bubbles or swirls as inclusions. Also chips have a typical shell like (conchoidal) rippled form.

Paste 'gem'. (Photo: KW)

The term 'paste' comes from the Italian name for dough and was used for the cheapest of glass fakes and is now applied to plastic copies as well.

'Rhinestones' is a term that has been used for many years to name any coloured glass imitation gemstone. The name comes from the French *caillou de Rhin*, referring to Strasbourg where the such gems were made. 'Diamanté' is a term used for bright coloured pastes used to decorate fabrics and may also be used to describe costume jewellery set with bright glass imitation stones, particularly in pavé style.

There are also natural glasses. The main variety being Obsidian, which was used extensively by the North American Indians and South American Aztecs for arrow heads or knives, due to the razor-sharp edges of the stone. It contains a high percentage (66 – 72%) of silica.

Obsidian is found in volcanic areas particularly in the Americas but also in Japan, Iceland, Hungary and Hawaii. Obsidian comes in a wide variety of colours and types. The commonest is black or grey, but red and blue have been reported.

Black material with white spots is called 'snowflake obsidian' whilst that banded red and black is 'mahogany obsidian'. Other small clear pebbles are romantically called 'Apache tears'. Obsidian is often used in local jewellery such as necklaces. Other types of natural glass occur but are rarely used in jewellery.

'Aventurine Glass' or 'Gold Stone' is a man-made material – a reddish-brown glass coloured by cuprous oxide that is treated to give masses of tiny copper crystals within the stone.

A recent newcomer into the costume jewellery market is a bright green glass coloured with depleted uranium; its radioactivity is far above safe limits! Extremely fluorescent under ultra-violet light, it is reported to emanate from the Czech Republic.

Uranium used to be used as a colouring agent in the manufacture of glass ornaments.

Tektite is a naturally-occurring glass of uncertain origin. Some believe that this was contained in meteorites, others that it was formed in rocks hit by hot meteorites.
Moldavite, named after Moldau in the Czech Republic

Snowflake obsidian. (Photo: KW)

where it was first discovered, is the only tektite that is transparent and suitable for faceting. In colour it is bottle green or brownish green. Tektites are found in other parts of the world, but rarely, if ever, of faceting quality.

Fake glass opal.
(Photo: KW)

Aventurine glass. (Photo: KW)

Plastics: almost all gemstones are now copied in plastic and, to the unwary, mounted stones may seem more realistic than one would imagine possible. They are of course much lighter even than glass. Remember that any genuine gemstone is set in a precious metal, plastic never.

Hematite necklace displayed on a piece of hematite ore. (Photo: AJ)

HEMATITE

Hematite, found in many places around the world including England, is, in fact, iron oxide. It was used in amulets in ancient Egypt and was believed by the Babylonians to "procure for the wearer a favourable hearing of petitions addressed to kings and a fortunate issue of lawsuits and judgments". A real boon in these litigious times. The variety used for jewellery is the crystalline form that has a blue-grey colour, when it is cut and polished it takes on a bright black metallic lustre. It has commonly been used for intaglios to be mounted in signet rings or pendants.

It is simulated by a material called 'hematine', which can be difficult to distinguish from natural hematite. Hematite is itself made into beads to simulate black pearls, though not very effectively as they are very heavy compared to the real thing. Some natural Brazilian hematite is magnetic.

It is approximately 6½ on the Mohs scale with an SG of approximately 5. If practicable it will give a red streak if rubbed on a unglazed porcelain tile. In fact, hematite becomes a bright red colour when crushed for use as a polishing agent, known as 'jeweller's rouge'.

Hematite. (Photo: DU)

HIDDENITE

Sister gem of Kunzite of the Spodumene group, hiddenite was first found in North California, USA and named after W.E. Hidden who worked that area.

Hiddenite. (Photos: KW)

It is a rich emerald green gem that is strongly pleochroic: yellowish-green, bluish-green and emerald green. The emerald green variety is extremely rare and must be classed as a collector's stone, but the paler shades are available. As kunzite, it is hard but brittle and difficult to cut, consequently it is not often used in jewellery.

IOLITE

An unusual gemstone, also known as Dichroite, but a worthy one nonetheless. The mineralogical name is Corderite.

It is a sapphire-blue in colour and competes with tanzanite as a cheaper alternative. It is strongly pleochroic showing yellow, light blue and dark violet-blue. It was once called 'water sapphire' but this term is now less common. It can be mistaken for sapphire but the pleochroism gives it away as with other similar look-a-likes.

It has a hardness of 7 to 7½ (Mohs) but is liable to chipping so the same care should be taken as with Tanzanite. The major sources of iolite are Sri Lanka, Myanmar (Burma), Madagascar (Malagasy Republic), S.W. Africa, Canada, Tanzania and India. Massive forms have been found and used for carvings.

Two examples of faceted iolite. Note the pleochroism in the example on the left. (Photo: MM)

JADE

Jade comes in two varieties – jadeite and nephrite, jadeite being the more valuable of the two.

Nephrite. (Photo: KW)

Jade medallion.
(Photo: RH)

Carved green jadeite. (Photo: RH)

Jadeite – Used by the Aztecs from sources in the Andes, jadeite was later discovered in Myanmar (Burma) about three hundred years ago and became popular with the Chinese emperors. Myanmar is still the major source today, although marketed through Hong Kong. More recently it has also been found in California and Russia, though not of gem quality.

Jadeite is found in a range of colours: bright green, purple, orange, brown, black and, very rarely, red. It varies from translucent to opaque; the most valuable is the bright translucent emerald green called 'Imperial Jade'. Next is the purple, the least popular colour is the dark olive green-grey. The more opaque the stone, the lower the value.

Off-colour jadeite is commonly dyed to simulate Imperial Jade but its opacity belies the truth. Improvement is also achieved by bleaching and impregnating with resin, although there are doubts as to the permanency of this procedure.

Jadeite with a hardness of 6½ to 7 and an SG of 3.33, is slightly harder than Nephrite but it is less tough. It has a bright glassy shine.

Most gems are cabochon cut and quite often waxed to improve the polish, but this may be damaged by heat and over zealous cleaning.

The latest classification of jadeite jade is-

'A' jade – natural untreated

'B' jade – polymer treated

'C' jade – stained

'B&C' jade – Polymer treated & stained

Nephrite – is found in very many locations around the world and is not used in jewellery as much as jadeite. It is used mainly for carvings. Brown shading of parts of the rock is

Jadeite. (Photo: Sotheby's)

caused by oxidation and this is used by carvers to attain a two-colour effect.

Nephrite jade comes in fewer colours than jadeite, white (mutton fat jade), dull green (spinach jade) often with black spots of magnetite, brilliant green and yellow, which is the most valuable.

Treatments are basically similar for nephrite as for jadeite: dyeing, waxing and bleaching are common.

It has a hardness of 6½ (Mohs) and an SG of approximately 3.0. It is an extremely tough material, which makes it difficult to mine. The main sources are now New Zealand, USA, Siberia, South America and Silesia.

There are very many simulants of jade: bowenite (a form of serpentine), chrysoprase, stained chalcedony, massive emerald, hydro-grossular garnet, amazonite, prehnite, Connemara marble and verde antique. Jade shows green under the Chelsea Filter where some simulants, particularly prehnite, show red. However, certain jades contain chromium and will also show red. This reinforces the doctrine of 'buy from a reliable source', not from street traders and make sure that the receipt states that it is genuine untreated jade.

Jadeite with ruby, sapphire and gold

In South America 'antique' jade articles are made from current jade and aged artificially by heat treatment to simulate the oxidation found on genuine old jade: very convincing.

KUNZITE

Kunzite, with its sister mineral hiddenite of the Spodumene group, is an attractive gem but more suitable for collectors.

Kunzite is a lilac-pink stone that is strongly pleochroic: violet, deep violet and colourless. It was originally discovered in California in 1902, but not of gem quality. A yellow-green variety that is of gem quality is found in the same location. Madagascar (Malagasy Republic), Afghanistan and Brazil, however, produce gem-quality lilac-pink kunzite.

Although it has a hardness of 7 (Mohs), it is fragile gem with a strong cleavage making it very difficult to cut. It is also subject to fading when exposed to strong light for long periods. Kunzite is not in general use but makes a cheap attractive addition to any collection.

Kunzite. (Photo: MM)

LAPIS LAZULI

The ancients knew lapis lazuli as 'sapphire' and it was not until the Middle Ages that blue corundum took over the use of that name. All the properties of a cure for diseases of the eye previously claimed for lapis lazuli were then transferred over to the more valuable gem, sapphire.

Lapis lazuli is in fact a mixture of different minerals, lazurite, hauynite, noselite, sodalite, calcite and pyrite. The best quality contains the least calcite and is found in Afghanistan and Russia. Lapis lazuli is also found in Chile but tends to be paler, containing bands of calcite and generally lacking the specks of golden pyrite that add to the attraction. It is also sourced from Myanmar (Burma) and USA.

Up until 1828 this beautiful blue mineral was crushed by artists to provide the pigment for ultramarine used for their paint; this is now produced synthetically.

Lapis lazuli is often used for signet rings and cuff links, though with a rating of only 5½ on the Mohs Scale it can easily be scratched.

Paler lapis is dyed to improve the colour but it is not necessarily stable. It is often waxed to improve the polish. The quartz mineral jasper is also dyed and called 'Swiss Lapis' or 'German Lapis'.

A synthetic sintered spinel, containing cobalt and which may contain gold specks, is produced in Germany to simulate lapis lazuli; it shows bright red under the

Chilean lapis. (Photo: KW)

Fabergé cigarette case. Gold, enamel lapis lazuli, c.1900. (Photo: WL)

Chelsea Filter where real lapis shows dull brownish-red. Gilson also produced a synthetic lapis lazuli. (See also Sodalite)

Afghan lapis lazuli. (Photo: AJ)

MALACHITE

Malachite, an important ore of copper, is a startling display stone. Large carvings and complete tabletops are made from this complex agate-like banded green mineral. Mined for thousands of years and long held precious as a talisman for the protection of children, it is as popular today as it has ever been. Occasionally set as ring stones or made into beads, its more usual use is in the manufacture of ornaments.

It has a hardness of only 4 on the Mohs scale, so is susceptible to damage. Its main source is the Congo, but good material is also found in Russia, Africa, Australia and New Mexico.

Azurite is a sister mineral of Malachite but is a lovely azure blue, hence the name. Both materials occur together and are often cut to display both in the same cabochon when it is termed 'azurmalachite'. It is also found together with the quartz mineral chrysocolla and, again, cut together.

Synthetic malachite has been produced in Russia but, due to malachite's low value, synthetics are not common.

Azurite. (Photo: KW)

Malachite. (Photo: KW)

A reconstructed material is sold in the form of ash trays and small bowls at Rock and Gem Shows.

A variety of azurite known as chessylite is found in France showing malachite bands.

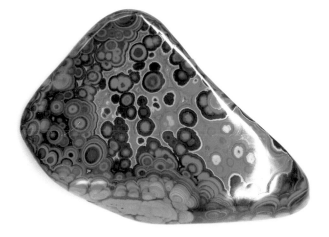

Malachite. (Photo: KW)

Azurite crystals. (Photo: KW)

Crystal of iron pyrites.
(Photo: KW)

Marcasite brooch. (Photo: KW)

MARCASITE

The 'gem' called Marcasite used in jewellery is in fact iron pyrites or 'fool's gold' and has been used for many centuries. The mineral marcasite, although chemically the same, is not suitable for use in jewellery. Popular with the Greeks and Incas alike large impressive crystal clusters are often found on sale as cabinet specimens.

Radial needle-like crystals of iron pyrites. (Photo: KW)

Pyrites is cut a bit like rose-cut diamonds and polished to a high shine. They are usually set with small beads gouged from the setting with a graver and folded over the edge of the stone. In cheaper jewellery they are set with adhesive. Pyrites form the pretty golden flecks in lapis lazuli.

It is liable to chipping if knocked so care is required in wearing and handling.

Marcasite jewellery tends to go in and out of fashion and is not as popular today as it was forty or fifty years ago. It is not expensive but is still simulated by cut steel, which has the disadvantage of rusting. Glass is also used but easy to identify.

True Marcasite can be found, with patience, in the chalk of the South Downs in England.

OPAL

Opal is a form of silica but different from quartz insomuch as it contains water in varying degrees. It is classed as a solidified jelly or gel. Its beauty comes from the display, in the form of flashes, of a rainbow of colours. There is a wide range of types but the only ones that need to concern us are as follows:

Precious Opal – this is the most expensive and is divided into three main classes: *black*, where the body colour is black, blue, green or grey; *light opal*, where the body colour is cream to white; and *clear* or *water opal*, which is clear with a good play of colour.

Black opal is ten times more expensive than light opal and consequently various treatments are applied to the latter to give the appearance of black.

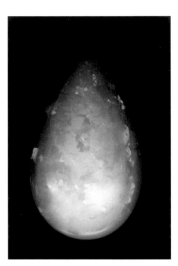

Opal doublet. (Photo: KW)

Fire opal. (Photo: MM)

Fire Opal – this is transparent or translucent orange to red, generally without a play of colour.

Jelly Opal or 'potch' – this is common opal that has no colour and is generally discarded.

Opal is different to most other gems in that it forms over a comparatively short timescale. It has even been found on the base of wooden fence posts. The main source of the gem is Australia, whose dealers give it a large number of descriptive names, based on the colour variations. Opals from the Yowah, Blackgate and Koroit areas are examples of opal in ironstone pebbles, these are polished and are unusual and attractive. Other sources are Hungary, USA and Brazil. Fire opal and water opal are found mainly in

Group of opals – including a black opal is at the top. (Photo: Christie's)

Opals and diamonds, c.1880. (Photo: WL)

Opals and diamonds, c.1900. (Photo: WL)

Mexico. A pink and blue opal without fire is found in Peru.

Doublets and triplets are common and, when in closed mounts, are difficult to detect. They are, or should be, cheaper than the solid stone. There is one advantage, however, with doublets: as opal is much softer than other

Natural black opal (left) alongside a Japanese synthetic. (Photo: AH)

gems (rating only 5½ to 6½ on the Mohs scale), a quartz-topped doublet will give protection.

As with any gemstone always purchase from a recommended source and avoid opals shown to you in water or oil.

Opal has also been synthesised and identification is not possible for the layperson. Gilson produced an excellent synthetic, but this has now been taken over by Chatham, following Gilsons closure. Other simulants are made from glass or plastic, but never look quite right. 'Slocum Stone' was developed in the USA as a convincing simulant, but Hong Kong remains the main source of imitation opal.

Opal is absorbent and will soak up water or any other liquid, so always take an opal ring off before doing the housework. They are also fragile so should be cleaned with care. A brief wash with a mild detergent in water is OK, but do not soak. As opals contain water, on average 10%, it is possible for them to dry out and crack, so heat should be avoided.

Peridot and diamond spider, c.1870. (Photo: WL)

PERIDOT

An attractive stone, peridot is the gem variety of the mineral olivine. A gem beloved by the Victorians, it is a yellowish-green in light and dark shades, some brownish. It is found in volcanic areas commonly in basalts. The classic locality is St John's Island in

Peridot. (Photo: Sotheby's)

the Red Sea, but it is also found in Arizona, Hawaii, Tanzania, China, Vietnam and the Canary Islands. Those from Hawaii sometimes contain inclusions of petrol.

Peridot rates 6½ on the Mohs scale, just below the recommended 7 for use in jewellery. Therefore it is liable to scratching or other damage if mounted high in a ring. Larger stones are to be preferred as the smaller ones fail to show the density of colour.

Peridot was frequently foil backed in antique jewellery to improve the colour of the lighter stones. Glass imitations are found, but do not show the double refraction of the natural stone.

Left: Cut peridot from St. Carlos, U.S.A.
(Photo: AJ)

Right: Group of peridots.
(Photo: AJ)

QUARTZ

Quartz is pure silica, which constitutes approximately 60% of the earth's crust: the sandy beach upon which we sit on holiday while the children build sand castles is quartz, as are the desert sands of the world.

Quartz is a large family consisting of two categories: crystalline and cryptocrystalline. The crystalline are those transparent gems that include amethyst, citrine, smoky quartz or cairngorm and rock crystal. The category of cryptocrystalline includes all the many translucent and opaque stones that are impure forms of the mineral.

Quartz also provides us with the most beautiful crystal clusters. Geodes, which are like bubbles formed during volcanic eruptions come in a variety of sizes. If you are lucky, when they are sliced in half a marvellous display of amethyst, citrine or other minerals greets your eye. Other delights are water agates that have water locked into their cavities that is millions of years old. When cut correctly the water can be seen through the stone moving about. In rare instances it can even be heard when the stone is shaken.

Crystalline (transparent) quartz:

Amethyst – this can range in colour from pale lilac to deep purple. The darker colours tend to be preferred and are consequently more expensive.

The main sources are Sri Lanka, USA, Brazil, Russia and Madagascar (Malagasy Republic). Nearer to home, it can also be found in the china clay pits of Cornwall,

Enamel and gold pendant by Falize set with amethyst, c.1880. (Photo: WL)

*Amethyst.
crystal cluster.*
(Photo: KW)

together with smoky quartz, but not of gem quality.

Even though supplies of natural amethyst are plentiful it is being synthesized. It can be very difficult to distinguish the new synthetics from the natural and, in fact, little effort is taken to sort the synthetic from the natural, due to its low value. A standard method to identify was to look for the 'thumbprint' inclusion that is diagnostic, but not all amethyst displays this. It looks, as it says, like a thumbprint or tiger stripes under the loupe.

Amethyst occurs in huge crystal-filled vugs or crevices, which are cut out for display. Some have legs and glass tops added to turn them into coffee tables.

Ametrine.
(Photo: DU)

Ametrine – this is where amethyst and citrine have blended together to produce a single bi-coloured gem. They are moderately priced but very attractive.

Cairngorm.
(Photo: KW)

Cartier brooch. Citrine and gold, c.1940. (Photo: WL)

Brown quartz: smoky quartz and cairngorm – Brown quartz is a transparent variety ranging in colour from pale to dark brown. Cairngorm gets its name from the Scottish mountain region where it was found; it was widely used in Celtic jewellery. This source is now exhausted and today's 'Cairngorm' is actually heat-treated amethyst from Brazil, similar to 'burnt amethyst'. The term 'smoky' is loosely applied to stones having a slightly cloudy look, although much brown quartz is still termed smoky. The sources are worldwide and the material is faceted in a range of styles as ring stones or beads.

Citrine – the majority of citrine is actually heat-treated amethyst called 'burnt amethyst'. The colour change is permanent, often banded, but lacks the dichroism of natural yellow quartz. However, if citrine is irradiated, it converts back to amethyst.

Citrine also comes in a range of shades from pale to dark yellow and brownish, where it merges into cairngorm or smoky quartz. It is often sold, wrongly, as yellow topaz but lacks the polish and brilliance. Clear quartz is now dyed to provide yellow shades and sold as citrine.

Despite their relatively low price, amethyst, ametrine and citrine stones make a lovely display in a range of jewellery.

Amethyst crystal surrounding a rock crystal core. (Photo: KW)

'Burnt Amethyst'. (Photo: KW)

Citrine. (Photo: KW)

Rock crystal – this is transparent colourless quartz that has been used as a diamond simulant, though not very convincingly. It is glasslike in appearance and can easily be confused with glass. Quartz, like most natural gems, has a higher thermal conductivity than glass; therefore the tongue test (as described under the section on diamond) should pick out the difference. It is important that the material being tested is are held with tweezers rather than held in the hand, to avoid accidentally warming it. The test is momentary so the quickest of touch should give a result i.e. the glass will feel warmer than the natural stone.

Rock crystal has often been the subject of large carvings in history and forms the best quality crystal balls used by fortune-tellers. In Sri Lanka it has long been used to make lenses for spectacles. It also has use in specialist lenses for optical instruments and as part of doublets and triplets.

Asteriated quartz occurs displaying 'stars' similar to ruby and sapphire. With correct lighting they can be very attractive. 'Venus Hair Stone' is quartz with needle-like inclusions of red or golden rutile, also called 'Fleches d'Amour'. It can occasionally contain black crystals of tourmaline. These can be found in Cornwall at Roche Rock.

'Bristol Diamonds', 'Herkimer Diamonds' and 'Saudi Diamonds' are all varieties of rock crystal named after the locations where they are found. The occurrence of rock crystal is very wide spread and large crystals for display are readily available. Synthetic quartz is also on the market in a range of colours.

Rose quartz – this is a common, massive form of quartz. Mostly cloudy, it is usually cut *en cabochon* for jewellery purposes. The deeper shades are the most popular, and the darker colours do show dichroism. Some examples are prone to fading. Star stones can be found. Stones, clean enough to be faceted, do turn up occasionally but are rare. It is regularly carved into

Rose quartz. (Photo. KW)

figurines and model animals etc.

Rose quartz is found in many parts of the world, the best coming from Brazil.

Cryptocrystalline (translucent) quartz:

The range of cryptocrystalline translucent and opaque quartz is huge. Many of the different types are used in a wide selection of jewellery.

Chalcedony – this cryptocrystalline quartz comes in a range of colours. A particularly attractive variety is the bright green *chrysoprase,* which is coloured by nickel; good quality examples can command a high price. A blue stone is also found and is well collected.

Chrysoprase. (Photo: KW)

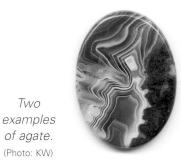

Two examples of agate. (Photo: KW)

Interestingly the flint that you find in chalk and on the beach is a poor quality chalcedony. Occasionally fossils may be found within the flint.

Agate is probably the best known of the chalcedony group. There is a wide range of patterns all given individual names. Most are banded: opaque bands alternating with transparent or translucent bands. As with all chalcedonies, agate is porous and so takes up dye well; it is regularly dyed bright colours. Although it is used in jewellery it is also used for many other

Mexican geode. (Photo: KW)

Agate and gold. (Photo: WL)

Two of the many patterns of agate: Sucor Creek (l.) and Apache Hills (r.). (Photo: KW)

Gold box with agate cameo lid, decorated with diamonds, c.1760. (Photo: WL)

Sardonyx. (Photo: KW)

Bloodstone (Heliotrope).
(Photo: KW)

Carnelian.
(Photo: KW)

purposes, such as table tops, clock faces and cameos. Popular for the latter are the brown and white banded stone, *sardonyx*, and the black and white banded stone, *onyx* (not to be confused with the onyx-marble, which is a completely different material). Many cameos are of course carved from shell.

Blue lace. (Photo: KW)

Other popular agates are moss agate, with inclusions that resemble plants, and landscape agate, where the inclusions give the appearance of a pictorial view of buildings.

Bloodstone or *Heliotrope* is an opaque dark green with splashes of red jasper. It got its name from the belief that it was the stone from below the cross of Christ, whose blood dropped upon it. NB. In Germany, 'Blutstein' [literally: bloodstone] is the name for hematite.

Carnelian or *cornelian* is a red form of chalcedony popular, among other things, for intaglio seals set into signet rings.

Chrome chalcedony is another prized green variety, coloured by chromium and showing red under the Chelsea Filter. Dyed material shows as a weak brownish red. Main sources are Bolivia and Zimbabwe.

Jasper is an opaque form of micro-crystalline (a compact mass of minute crystals) quartz that is strongly coloured by other minerals, mainly iron. Red, yellow, brown and green are fairly common; bright reds are prized and used for inlay and carvings. It has many varieties and it is found worldwide.

Tiger's eye – this is an attractive golden-brown opaque stone displaying a cat's eye effect. The effect is caused by asbestos inclusions. A blue variety is known as 'Hawk's-eye'.

Tiger's eye
(Photo: KW)

Rhodochrosite brooch.
(Photo: KW)

Rhodonite.
(Photo: KW)

RHODOCHROSITE

A dainty, attractive, pink-and-white banded, translucent stone: it looks almost like a candy sweet. Rarely clear crystals do occur, though these are very small. Unfortunately this stone only has a hardness of 4, but is quite suitable for wear in pendants or brooches.

Originally found in Argentina, it was believed to be used by the Incas, indeed it is sometimes called 'Rosinca' or 'Inca Rose'. It only came into modern use in the late 1940s when it was rediscovered by amateur lapidaries during the rock hunting craze, which peaked in the 1960s and '70s. It has been found in the USA, Romania, Hungary, India and the Saxony region of Germany.

RHODONITE

This stone is similar in coloration to rhodochrosite but with black marbling. Less common than rhodochrosite, it is also harder, registering 6 on the Mohs Scale. Red transparent crystals of gem quality are occasionally found, but are rare.

As it occurs in massive form it is generally used for carvings and ornaments. Rhodonite is believed by crystal healers to bring emotional stability.

It was first discovered in the Urals in the eighteenth century, but these deposits are now virtually worked out. It is now sourced mainly from the USA, Sweden, South Africa and Australia. It has also been found in Cornwall, UK.

Rhodochrosite and rhodonite compared.
(Photo: AJ)

SERPENTINE

The most common form of serpentine encountered is the massive opaque variety, which forms rocky outcrops and is found in several localities including around the Lizard in Cornwall. It is generally found in shades of green but it has a wide variation, sometimes with red blotches of bastite. The veined appearance is believed to have given rise to its name. It is mainly used for ornamental carvings. It is comparatively very soft, at 2½ on the Mohs Scale.

The more desirable variety is *bowenite*, a translucent yellowish green with a greasy lustre. This may be mistaken for jade, except that it is much softer, registering 4 on the Mohs scale. Small inclusions of bowenite have been found with the common type of serpentine in Cornwall.

It was used by the Maoris of New Zealand where it was found on the South Island.

Other sources are China, Afghanistan, India, Russia (Zmeevik) and the USA. Both forms are found in South Africa. Italy has produced some excellent serpentine marbles.

The West coast of Eire produces a variety named 'Connemara Marble' or 'Irish Green' marble, this is a paler green with white veining. It is used locally for jewellery in a wide range of designs.

SOAPSTONE

Soapstone is the massive variety of steatite or talc. Powdered and perfumed it is what we use on ourselves after a shower. It is very soft and can be scratched with a fingernail.

It is widely spread and popular for carving particularly in China, India and South Africa. Pure it is white, but impurities may make it green, brown, yellow or reddish. It has a greasy feel and is quite light in weight. It is popular as a tourist souvenir, and the carvings are often found at gem shows.

Cornish serpentine.
(Photo: KW)

Bowenite (at the top of the stone) with serpentine.
(Photo: KW)

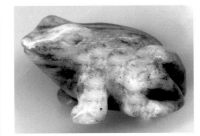

Connemara marble. (Photo: KW)

Soapstone carving
(Photo: KW)

69

Sodalite cabochon. (Photo: KW)

SPINEL

Spinel is an important gemstone in its own right, though it is somewhat overshadowed by ruby and sapphire. It is of the cubic system and, consequently, singly refractive; an identifying feature. Deep red, it is sometimes called 'Balas Ruby'; a famous example is the 'Black Prince's Ruby' set in the English Crown Jewels, which is, in fact, a spinel. Deep reds command a high price, whereas the paler shades of red, brownish and yellowish reds are much cheaper. Pale to deep blue, violet blue, purple and mauve are also important.

It is hard, 8 on the Mohs scale of hardness, with a vitreous or glassy lustre, capable of a high polish. Sources are many: Myanmar (Burma), Sri Lanka, Afghanistan, Thailand, Australia, Sweden, Brazil and the USA.

Synthetic spinel has been produced commercially for very many years. It is made in colours not usual for natural spinel: blues simulating aquamarine and zircon,

SODALITE

Sodalite can be one of the constituent minerals of lapis lazuli, but is often cut as a gem itself. It is an attractive blue stone marbled with white and may also be confused with lapis. It is also found in other colours but only the strong blue is used. It never reaches the ultramarine of lapis but the royal blue is very striking. It has also been called 'Canadian Bluestone'. Occasionally flecks of pyrites are found in the stones.

Originally discovered in commercial quantity in Canada, it has subsequently been found in several other areas of the world: the USA, Norway, India, Brazil and British Columbia.

It has hardness of 5½ to 6 on the Mohs scale. It is tricky to cut due to a strong cleavage, but polishes into very attractive cabochons for pendants and brooches. It is also fashioned into beads and even into larger items such as boxes and clock cases.

Spinel dress studs. (Photo: AJ)

Synthetic spinel boules and the resulting cut stones. (Photo: RH)

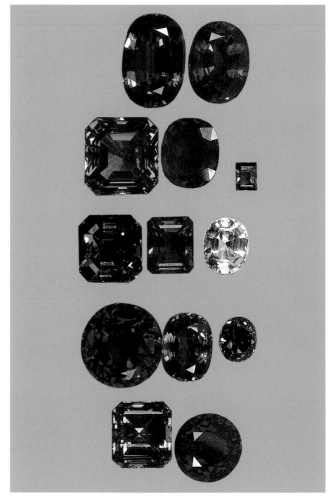

Various colours of spinel. (Photo: AJ)

TANZANITE

Discovered at the Mererani mines of Tanzania in 1967, this gem is a variety of Zoisite. In nature it occurs in several colours, but all are usually heat treated to attain the beautiful violet blue that originally attracted the interest in this gem. A deep blue, which may be confused with sapphire, is expensive.

Although of acceptable hardness, it is also somewhat fragile and ultra-sonic cleaning should be avoided. Use as a ring stone should be considered with care.

Tanzanite is strongly dichroic, showing red-violet and deep blue depending on the direction viewed. A green variety in gem quality has also been discovered.

It has been very strongly marketed, pale colours of less appeal appearing on TV shopping channels. However, supplies of good material are dwindling.

The Tanzanite Foundation has produced the Tanzanite Quality Scale (see Appendix 5), a grading system similar to that of diamond, covering colour, clarity and cut.

Other grading systems have been quoted on shopping channels but carry no validity. Prices vary considerably; the higher the degree of violet saturation, the greater the value.

There are several simulants including synthetic corundum and synthetic garnet. As yet, Tanzanite itself has not been synthesized.

both showing a strong red under the Chelsea Filter. It is also used to simulate alexandrite and, of course, sapphire. A colourless variety is produced to simulate diamond but is not very successful as it lacks the fire when brilliant cut, so is often cut as baguettes.

Tanzanite. (Photo: RH)

Russian pink topaz and diamonds, c.1870. (Photo: WL)

Blue topaz.
(Photo: Christie's)

Imperial topaz.
(Photo: RH)

White topaz.
(Photo: KW)

Pink topaz. (Photo: MM)

TOPAZ

Topaz occurs in yellow, pink (rare), colourless and the prized sherry yellow 'Imperial Topaz'. The major source is Brazil, but it is also found in Australia, Russia, Sri Lanka, Myanmar (Burma) and the USA. It has also been reported in the British Isles.

It has a vitreous lustre and is very slippery to the touch. It is also quite fragile due to its tendency to develop fractures, it will even crack and break if knocked; this applies to all colours. You may also find inclusions if you look closely: tiny liquid-filled cavities or small crystals. This is what makes gemmology such a fascinating subject. Of course, the fewer the inclusions and 'cleaner' the stone, the better.

As yet, topaz has not been commercially synthesised but it can easily be confused with certain simulants: yellow quartz, citrine (sometimes labelled as 'Scottish Topaz'), yellow beryl, tourmaline and yellow corundum ('Oriental Topaz'). 'Synthetic Topaz' is actually synthetic corundum or spinel.

Brazilian topaz, c.1840. (Photo: WL)

Blue topaz comes from irradiated or heat-treated colourless material. Depending on the length of the treatment, a range of shades is produced from a light blue to a dark sky-blue called 'London Blue'. Colourless topaz is in plentiful supply; it was commonly used as a diamond simulant, though, since the success of the treatments, most is now used to produce the popular blue topaz.

A range of coated topaz has also been produced over recent years; this is mostly pink or green, but is also available with an iridescent titanium coating called 'Mystic Fire' or 'Mystic Topaz'. There are doubts about its durability.

TOURMALINE

This gem is, in fact, one of the most interesting. It exists in a wide range of colours each with its own name:

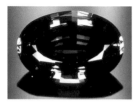

Dravite. (Photo: RH)

Indicolite. (Photo: RH)

Rubellite. (Photo: MM)

Schorl crystal. (Photo: KW)

Green tourmaline.
(Photo: RH)

Watermelon tourmaline. (Photo: MM)

Achroite – colourless.

Chrome Tourmaline – green, containing chromium; may be mistaken for emerald.

Dravite – brown.

Indicolite – blue; has been passed off as sapphire. The yellow variety from Kenya has been sold as yellow sapphire.

Rubellite – red; in the deeper shades has been mistaken for ruby.

Schorl – black; was used for mourning jewellery.

Other varieties – green is the most common colour and ranges in shade from very pale to dark. A new variety was discovered in Brazil in 1987 that is a transparent, intense blue or bluish green. These are

Gold brooch set with a large red tourmaline surrounded by diamonds in the form of a snake. This was a gift from Edward VII to Mrs Keppell, c.1890. (Photo: WL)

known as **Paraiba** or **Neon Tourmaline** and command extremely high prices.

Sometimes crystals form where the colours are in layers around the length of the crystal. In some the centre is pink and the outer green with a colourless layer in between. When a cross section of the crystal is cut it is known as a **Watermelon Tourmaline**. Very attractive, but also expensive.

Tourmaline occurs in Brazil, Russia, USA, Africa, India, Pakistan and Sri Lanka. Like quartz, tourmaline displays pyroelectric effects (upon heating, an electric charge is induced with opposite polarity at each end of the crystal) and piezoelectric effects (when under pressure an electrical charge is induced).

Tugtupite cabochon. (Photo: AH)

Veined turquoise. (Photo: KW)

Natural untreated turquoise from Iran.
(Photo: KW)

TUGTUPITE

An unusual name for an unusual stone: discovered in Greenland and approved as a gemstone in 1963, its name means 'Reindeer Stone'. It is carved locally for small ornaments and jewellery.

Shades include orange, pink and bright red. Unusually, when kept in the dark, the pale shades fade to white, but recover their colour when exposed to daylight. It is doubly refractive with a hardness of around 6.5, depending on impurities.

Although mainly found in its massive form, occasionally transparent specimens are found that may be faceted. It is still mainly sourced from Greenland, though it is also found in northwest Russia and Canada.

It is strongly fluorescent under ultra-violet light and may also fluoresce in strong sunlight.

Tugtupite is said by the Inuit to glow a bright red, indicating the depth of lovers' feelings for each other.

TURQUOISE

Turquoise has been used as decoration for thousands of years. It was highly prized by the Persians when first discovered. The Ancient Egyptians found it in the Sinai Peninsula: a huge mining operation involving 8,000 men took place there seven thousand years ago. It was also used by the Aztecs and by the North American Indians.

In the Middle Ages the Venetians gave it the name 'Turksea', meaning 'Turkey Stone', because although originating from Persia (now Iran), it was sourced through Turkey; and hence turquoise.

The turquoise from Persia has the clearest sky blue and is still classed as the finest, while that from Egypt has a greenish tinge. Other sources are New Mexico and California in the USA, and China. A veined variety is found around Medina in Saudi Arabia and is used in Bedouin jewellery.

Turquoise has also been found near Liskeard in Cornwall, England, but only as a collector's specimen. A hardness of only 6 on the Mohs scale does make it liable to abrasion. 'Spider web' patterns across the stone distract from its value, although some people prefer to see it. It has remained a popular gem and is widely used.

Gold brooch, given by Queen Victoria to one of her bridesmaids. Turquoise, pearls and cabochon rubies. (Photo: WL)

Due to its variable fragility it is often 'stabilised' by impregnating with wax or plastic under pressure. It is also reconstituted by bonding pulverised turquoise, after removal of any impurities, into slabs that may be cut into gems.

It is simulated by glass, porcelain and plastic that may be identified by careful inspection with the loupe, which will show small bubbles. Dyed chalcedony or howlite are used as simulants but the former has a glassy lustre. It has also been synthesised by Gilson, now taken over by Chatham, but is expensive.

Unakite. (Photo: KW)

UNAKITE

An uncommon mineral sometimes offered mounted in jewellery. It is a form of granite consisting of quartz, pink feldspar and green epidote. It is opaque, but when polished produces an attractive stone.

Unakite takes its name from the region where it is found, the Unaka mountain range in North Carolina, USA. It is also found in other regions of the USA, Zimbabwe and in Galway Bay, Eire.

Brooch by Giuliano. Coloured zircons and diamonds, c.1890. (Photo: WL)

ZIRCON

Among the heaviest of gemstones the zircon only reached popularity in the 1920s. It was later found that when heat-treated it produced a beautiful blue.

Unfortunately these stones tend to fade, but reheating can restore the colour. In their natural state, zircons are usually yellow, orange, brown, greenish brown and olive green.

White zircon, (also due to heat treatment) having a high refractive index and fire, competes with diamond in its brilliance and has been used as a simulant.

Zircon is readily identifiable to the practised eye, but not necessarily to the amateur. It has a very high double refraction that can be noted under the loupe, which of course diamond does not.

One unusual property of zircon is that it is faintly radio-active, though not at a level that it is harmful.

Zircon has had several names applied to it in the past, including 'jargoon' or 'cerkonier'. Yellowish-red and orange-red were called 'hycinth' and 'jacinth' (see the 'Most Noble Electuary of Jacinth' on p.17).

Zircon. (Photo: AJ)

Care should be taken when handling these gems as they are somewhat brittle and the facet edges can get damaged.

Zircon is simulated by synthetic blue spinel, but is easily distinguished as zircon has large double refraction, whereas spinel is singly refractive.

Zircon is prolific in the gem gravels of Sri Lanka and in Myanmar (Burma). Red crystals are found near Le Puy in France. It is also found in the USA, Australia, Cambodia and Thailand.

Organic Gems

AMBER

Amber is the fossilised resin of Pine trees – mainly the *Pinus succinifera,* which thrived over thirty million years ago. Amber is mostly to be found in Russia, the shores of the Baltic Sea, and is washed up in Norway, Denmark and the East coast of the British Isles.

Amber appears in various colours: yellow, brown, reddish, green and white. It has a hardness of about 2 and a greasy lustre.

Although most amber is washed up along the various coasts there is a variety that is open-mined in Russia termed 'pit amber'. It produces small pieces, which are pressed together and termed 'Venetian Amber', 'Compressed Amber' or 'Ambroid'.

A major source of tropical amber is found in the mudstone mines of Amber Valley in the Dominican Republic, where amber was originally cherished by the native Taino tribes but forgotten until being 'rediscovered' in the 1960s.

In Greece, amber was called 'electron' because, when rubbed with a cloth, a negative electrical charge is induced that attracts small pieces of paper or other light material.

In Germany it is called 'Bernstein' where it is powdered and burnt as incense.

Sometimes it is possible to find insects trapped in the

Silver bracelet set with three colours of amber.
(Photo: JH)

Shades of Baltic amber as found. (Photo: MCP)

amber and these pieces are most collectable, but – and a very big BUT – there are a lot of fakes about. Copal resin, which is a recent fossil resin, is almost identical and is the most popular simulant used in these copies. In nature, an insect, trapped in a drop of amber resin as it dripped down the bark of the tree, had time to wriggle before it set. This may show as swirl marks around the moving parts of the poor imprisoned creature. In the fakes dead insects are planted into copal resin and, consequently, there are no swirl marks.

An easy way to tell amber and copal resin apart is to test with ether: a spot of ether will have no effect on real amber, but will leave a sticky patch on copal resin.

Other simulants are glass, bakelite, celluloid, casein and perspex. Again, detection is not difficult if the stone is not mounted. Mix up a saline solution in a glass of water, about two or three teaspoons of salt should do according to the size of the glass. True amber will float, these other simulants, which have a greater specific gravity, will sink.

Polystyrene has almost the same SG as amber but is attacked by toluene.

One room in the palace at St Petersburg in Russia had a room entirely panelled in amber. Unfortunately the panelling disappeared during the second world war, but it has now been completely recreated.

Fly trapped in Dominican amber. (Photo: MCP)

Polished ammolite. (Photo: Korite)

Ammolite and gold pendant. (Photo: SB)

AMMOLITE

Ammolite is the mineralised remains of the *Ammonite Placenticeras* – a hard shelled squid-like sea creature from the Upper Cretaceous period, sixty-five million years ago. Its name was taken from the Egyptian god Ammon. Ammonite fossils are fairly common worldwide; they are prolific on the beaches of Lyme Regis in England. However, the variety used as a gem because of its beautiful colours, occurs only in the Canadian Province of Southern Alberta. It was classified as a gemstone by the Coloured Stone Commission in 1981. Its appearance is similar to black opal with a spectacular display of interference colours.

It is comparatively rare and expensive. It is very friable and subject to damage. It is therefore sold as doublets or triplets, the face being protected with a dome of synthetic spinel or quartz. The base of the triplets is usually a natural shale. Unprotected ammolite must be treated with even more care than opal, not being worn when it may be knocked or when liable to become wet. Cleaning should only be done with a barely damp cloth without soaking. even as a doublet or triplet it should not be soaked.

The exponents of Feng Shui believe that ammolite absorbs cosmic energy, which is then given off to the owner – bringing health, wealth and enlightenment. It was used as an amulet by native Americans against evil spirits.

CORAL

Precious coral used for jewellery is not, in fact, the coral that builds enormous reefs in the South Seas but a particular variety called *Corallium Rubrum* or *Corallium Nobile*.

Coral polyps are a plant-like animal and are extremely small, barely 2 millimetres in diameter. They are a bit like a small sea anemone but their external skeletons mass together to form tree like structures. Precious

Coral and gold cross by John Brogden, c.1870.

(Photo: WL)

coral is found around the Mediterranean, the Red Sea, Malay Archipelago and Japan.

The most valuable colours are very dark red (ox blood) through to pink. Most of the fashioning of coral is in Italy, where cameos, cabochons and beads are cut. It is very beautiful but very soft: only 3½ on the Mohs Scale. It contrasts extremely well with turquoise. Being composed of calcium carbonate it is readily attacked by acids.

It is only to be expected that precious coral has many simulants. Stained vegetable ivory (see Ivory) is used but can be identified by the dot like cell structure under the loupe. Glass, plastic and porcelain are also used. Pale coloured coral is also dyed to improve its appearance, but the dye will come off with nail polish remover.

Black coral, which is composed of conchiolin rather than calcite, is found in the Indian Ocean, Hawaii, West Indies and the Pacific Islands. This is also fashioned into jewellery. Its export is banned from several countries.

Coral has been used as talismans for thousands of years, but was believed to retain its powers only if it remained unworked. Red and white coral are both said to give safety to the wearer during storms and tempests.

Red coral brooch.
(Photo: Sotheby's)

Pink coral, diamond and gold earrings. (Photo: Sotheby's)

HORN

Although horn is at the very borders of our subject of gems it is worth noting that various types of animal horn are used in carvings and inlay and, occasionally, jewellery.

Deer or, more correctly, stag horn is in popular use having a hardness of 2½ on the Mohs scale. Buffalo horn is also used in the developing countries for tourist souvenirs. Scarab beetles carved from horn are found in Egypt, suitably inscribed with hieroglyphs. In India horn is fashioned into carved boxes.

Heart-shaped horn box, from India. (Photo: KW)

Horn scarab marked with hieroglyphs, from Egypt. (Photo: KW)

'Engine-turning' markings in elephant ivory. (Photo: MCP)

The import and sale of ivory is illegal in the UK and several other countries. The only ivory allowed in is 'antique' (pre-1947) or fossil ivory carrying an authenticating document.

Carved ivory pendant. (Photo: ACC)

IVORY

Ivory comes from different sources: we immediately connect it with elephant tusks, but it is also from the narwhale, mammoth (fossil), hippopotamus, walrus, boar and the cachalot whale. A gemmologist can identify each different type of ivory, but this is unnecessary for the amateur.

Strictly speaking, ivory is dentine, the same as all mammal teeth - even our own! The difference is that our teeth have a coating of enamel, whereas ivory, such as elephant tusks, does not. Elephant ivory is identified by patterning that sometimes occurs, which looks like engine-turning marks.

Bone is the most common simulant but is identifiable by a series of canals, which upon inspection under the loupe, appear as short, broken, dark lines or little oval or circular spaces. Deer or stag horn is also used, its markings bear a resemblance to bone but are less defined.

'Vegetable ivory' is made from the

Bone bracelet, note the canals.
(Photo: JH)

nuts of the Ivory Palm (*Phytelephas macrocarpa*), known as Corozo or Tagua Nuts, from South America. Its hardness is the same as true ivory, making a convincing simulant, particularly when carved. It was imported in large quantities in the 19th century and used for buttons, chess pieces and jewellery. The Doom Palm (*Hyphaene thebaica*), from North and Central Africa, also a produces a nut used to make an ivory simulant but it is less hard than the corozo nut. Both these nuts can be stained successfully. Celluloid is also used to imitate ivory, and makes effective fakes. Other plastics are not as convincing.

Ivory from the fossilised tusks of mammoths found in Alaska and the Yukon is marketed freely in Canada and the USA. Complete tusks, when found, are not cut for jewellery but sent to museums.

Carved ivory brooch (Photo: ACC)

Carved Whitby jet. (Photo: MCP)

Rough jet, as found. (Photo: KW)

JET

Jet is the fossilised wood of prehistoric trees that have been compressed over millions of years. It was known and worked long before the Romans came to England. They, in fact, were so delighted with it that they shipped large quantities back to Rome. It was mined from the coastal areas around Whitby in Yorkshire where it occurred in seams in the rock between one to six inches thick; it could also be collected from the beaches.

This dense black material in the form of beads, pendants and charms has been found in early burial mounds across the British Isles. The Victorians continued this association and upon the death of Prince Albert jet mourning jewellery proliferated. It became so popular that the local supply was supplemented by material from Spain to be worked in the Whitby workshops.

Jet is also found in France, Germany, the USA and Russia, although it does not appear to have been worked to any great extent.

Jet is soft, rating just 2½ on Mohs scale, so is easily carved. It takes a high polish in the hands of the skilled craftsmen.

Although the jet industry in Whitby has declined considerably since Victorian days, it is still a popular tourist attraction in Whitby where jet jewellery may still be purchased.

Simulants abounded over the years, black glass ('Paris Jet') being common, but easily distinguished by its weight. Scottish cannel coal, vulcanite and plastics have also all been used. The usual test is to use a hot needle applied to an inconspicuous part of the suspect material: plastics and vulcanite will give off the characteristic smell of chemical or rubber, jet will smell of coal.

Recently, models have appeared in the tourist shops that may have the look of dull jet and are marked 'Made of Coal'. They are, indeed, a compressed coal dust and not jet.

PEARLS

Pearls are the moon to the diamond's sun. They have been held in esteem for thousands of years; highly valuable, strings of them graced the necks and garments of kings and queens. A gem not produced by the high temperatures and pressures in the depths of our planet, but grown in the shell of a simple sea creature: the oyster.

A pearl is produced when a foreign body enters the oyster between the mantle and the shell – which must be a bit like having a stone in your shoe. The animal cures the aggravation by coating it with a substance called nacre, which keeps growing into a pearl.

In the 1890s a Japanese pedlar of noodles, Kokichi Mikimoto started the commercial production of Cultured Pearls after many years of experimentation. The idea of accelerating the process of pearl production was not new. The Chinese began inserting objects into freshwater mussels in the thirteenth century, but it wasn't until Mikimoto appeared that they became a real threat to natural pearls. Nowadays 90% of pearls sold are 'cultured'.

Pearls are valued by size, shape, flawlessness, colour and lustre.

Size – pearls are measured by weight in grains: there are 4 grains to the carat. That is the same carat by which all gems are weighed. However, it is not uncommon now for pearls to be quoted in millimetres.

Japanese cultured pearls. Sizes, from the left, 2mm, 3mm, 4mm, 5mm, 6mm, 7mm, 8mm, 9.5mm, 10.5mm. Shown actual size. (Photo: ACC)

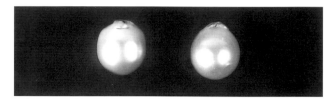

Pair of South Sea pearls showing a growth formation. Shown actual size. (Photo: ACC)

Shape – The ideal shape for a pearl is perfectly round, though natural pearls are quite often imperfect. Cultured pearls, however, are usually round due to the way they are formed. Odd shaped pearls are called 'baroque' and are particularly common in the freshwater variety.

'Blister pearls', formed when the growing nacre is attached to the shell, are usually shaped in a hemisphere. These are cut from the surface of the shell and set where the underside is hidden by the mounting. They may also be filled with a paste after removing the interior and covered with a mother-of-pearl backing. These are called Mabé pearls.

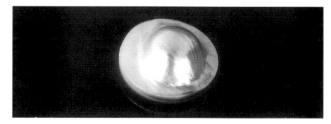

Mabé pearl cut from the inner surface of the oyster shell. This will be trimmed before being set. Shown actual size. (Photo: ACC)

Flawlessness – just as it implies, this refers to the pearl having no imperfections its the surface. Only three flaws will reduce a pearl's value by 50%. Sometimes these marks are hidden by the drilling of the bead.

Colour – Pearls come in a variety of colours and shades, depending on the source. Those from the Arabian Gulf tend to be creamy-white, whereas those from Australia are silver-white or yellow.

Lustre – this is known as the 'orient' of the pearl and is what gives it its unique beauty and value. Also termed 'iridescence', it is caused by refraction of light through the many layers of nacre.

To correct a misconception, pearls are obtained from the pearl oyster (*Pinctada*) not the edible one you have in a restaurant. They are also found in abalone, producing green, yellow, blue and black pearls, and in the great conch, producing pink pearls. These are generally found in the Gulf of California.

The pearl oyster, abalone and great conch are all sea creatures and therefore produce salt-water pearls. Freshwater pearls are produced by mussels.

Mississippi pearls were popular around the beginning of the twentieth century. They were found in the northern reaches of the Mississippi river in the fresh water mussel, mostly prized for its mother-of-pearl. The pearls are generally baroque in shape and come in a variety of colours.

Detail of a Tiffany brooch. Mississippi pearls and diamonds, c.1900 (Photo: WL)

German brooch. Conch pearl and diamonds, c.1900.
(Photo: WL)

Cultured pearl, cross-section. Note the mother-of-pearl bead core and the skin of nacre grown around it. The thicker this skin, the better quality the cultured pearl.
(Photo: KW)

Cultured Pearls – these are mainly produced using salt-water oysters. The process, in the simplest terms, consists of placing a bead of mother-of-pearl (usually between 6 and 13 mm in diameter) between the mantle and the shell of a live oyster in a laboratory and returning it to the oyster beds to grow. The length of time that they are left to grow determines the eventual quality of the final product. Several years ago they would be left for two years or more to grow their coating of nacre but commercial pressure has reduced the growing time to six to eight months. Consequently, many cultured pearls have a very thin layer of nacre that tends to wear away or peel off. Better-quality pearls, sourced from the South Seas, are still available, but at a price. They are generally larger than the Japanese Akoya pearl.

Cultured pearls are also produced in a range of colours and some are dyed, particularly black pearls. Tahiti provides most of the coloured pearls and these are also larger than the Japanese pearls. The birthplace of the cultured pearl, Japan is now the main marketing centre for the gem. The principle product is now the Akoya pearl.

Simulated Pearls – these have been produced for hundreds of years: it is believed that many of the pearls that adorned the costumes of Queen Elizabeth the First were artificial.

One of the best simulated pearls is the 'Majorica', produced in Majorca, it was introduced in 1953 and is very difficult to distinguish from both the natural and the cultured pearl. The base is a glass bead, which is coated with a solution of powdered fish scales and bismuth oxychloride to give the iridescent quality. The complete process is a closely guarded secret.

Cheap copies are also made and sold in Majorca but they do not have to same lustre and beauty.

Simulants were also made in Czechoslovakia and France during the twenties and thirties using wax-filled hollow glass beads and fish scales but tended to be dull when compared with a real or good cultured pearl. The flood of cheap cultured pearls has had severe repercussions on the market for simulants.

The standard test for whether a pearl is genuine or a simulant is to gently rub it against the edge of your top teeth, a real pearl will feel rough whereas a fake will feel smooth. This test will not identify a cultured pearl, however, as these also feel rough.

A natural pearl will always have a good lustre and may identify it from a cheaper cultured pearl. If you look closely at the hole in a bead where the thread goes through, the coating of the cultured pearl may show signs of wearing away around the edge of the hole.

Freshwater pearls – these are farmed in rivers and lakes. Japan began development of freshwater pearls using clams in the 1930s at Lake Biwa, which were first marketed in 1961. Unfortunately pollution of the lake eventually halted production.

Most, if not all, freshwater pearls are non-nucleated, meaning that instead of a mother-of-pearl bead being inserted into the mollusc a small piece of mantle is introduced instead. The pearl grown is 80-90% pure nacre. The Chinese have now taken up the production of the pearls and are the major supplier with varying degrees of quality. Mussels are used in many places of the world, including Scotland, to produce pearls: strings of baroque (non-uniform shape) freshwater pearls are available quite cheaply at gemshows.

Cultured oyster pearls. (Photo: RH)

Range of Chinese cultured non-nucleated mussel pearls of varying quality. (Photo: MCP)

SHELL

Abalone or **Paua Shell** – used extensively for costume jewellery, it is easily identified by the iridescent play of colour and swirling patterns. It is found mainly around New Zealand and Queensland, Australia, as well as California and Florida in the U.S.A. It also produces pearls in green, yellow, blue and black.

Mother-of-Pearl – produced from the shell of the large pearl oyster, this has been used for many years for the manufacture of buttons, inlays, knife handles, gaming counters etc. It is often dyed.

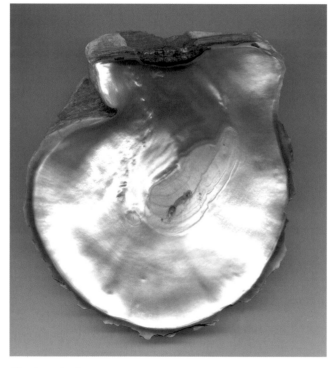

Oyster shell. (Photo: KW)

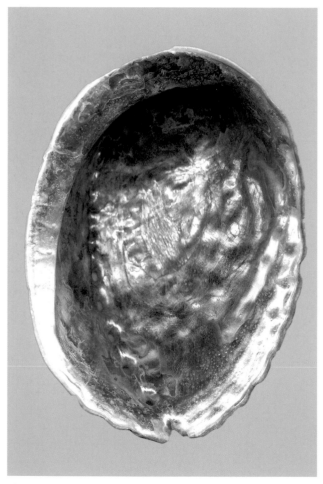

Abalone shell. (Photo: KW)

Louis XV gold snuff box inlaid with mother-of-pearl. (Photo: WL)

Shell cameo, a relief carving of Poseidon, God of Seas and Oceans. c.1870. (Photo: MR)

Helmet Shell – this large shell of the *Cassis madagascariensis* is commonly used for the production of cameos. The cameos are white relief on a brown background. The giant conch is also used for cameos giving a white relief on a rose-coloured background, which has a tendency to fade. Both are found in the waters around the West Indies.

Operculum (Latin for 'little lid') – also known as the 'Chinese cat's-eye', this is actually the trap-door of the winkle; but not the small edible kind. It comes from a large snail-like mollusc *Turbo petholatus*. The operculum can range from a ¼ inch to 3 inches in diameter. The top is domed and is green, white and brown; the underside is flat. When the mollusc retires

Operculum. (Photo: KW)

into its shell the operculum closes behind him. Operculum is found around the islands off Singapore and the Phillipines. They have been used as eyes for grotesque statues and, on Stewart Island off New Zealand, as a form of currency.

Shell cameo. (Photo: Sotheby's)

Tortoiseshell – this actually comes from a sea turtle, the Hawksbill Turtle, rather than a tortoise. It got its rather misleading name 'tortoiseshell' when family groupings were not as advanced as today and the two creatures were still confused. The source of the best shell is the East Indies but it is also found in West Indies, Brazil and Malay Archipelago.

Tortoiseshell is thermoplastic, which means that it softens and becomes pliable under heat, rendering it possible to flatten and smooth the curved plates of the turtle's shell. Sheets are also joined by 'welding' them together with heat and pressure.

Tortoiseshell has been used as facings for furniture, inlays, spectacle frames, combs ... a myriad of different articles. Precious metals and brass (as in 'Boule' furniture) are sometimes inlaid in the surface of the shell by placing them on the top and pressing them into the warmed tortoise-shell.

The amber or yellow colour is marked with darker patches that, when inspected under the loupe, show up as a series of dots; a bit like a photo in a newspaper. The closer the dots the darker the patch. This distinguishes it from the plastic simulant where the mottling is in swathes and bands not dots. Blonde shell from the belly plates is also used but this does not have the mottling.

As with most organic materials, it has a hardness of 2½ according to the Mohs scale.

The import and sale of tortoiseshell is illegal in the UK and several other countries. The only tortoiseshell allowed in is antique and must be carrying an authenticating document.

Plastic 'tortoiseshell'.
(Photo: KW)

Antique tortoiseshell card case inlaid with mother-of-pearl.
(Photo: KW)

Tortoiseshell and gold piqué, c.1740. (Photo: WL)

A Selection of Minor Gemstones

The term 'minor' does not reflect the monetary value of these stones rather their rarity as regards their use in jewellery: most can be classed as "collectors' stones". However, in the present climate of introducing new gems to the public, it is possible that they may occasionally be offered over the internet or the TV shopping channels.

ALBITE (H.7) – a colourless variety of feldspar.

AMBLYGONITE (H.5.5-6) – a soft stone in a variety of colours, commonly included, cut mainly for collectors.

ANGLESITE (H.2.5-3) – a very soft stone, occasionally in yellow, blue or green, but usually colourless. Being a lead mineral it is very heavy with an S.G. of 6.3+. Cut for collectors.

APATITE (H.5) – occurs in yellow, green, blue, violet & colourless transparent crystals. With a hardness of only 5 it is vulnerable to damage unless set considerately. It can be very attractive and has a vitreous lustre. The pale green variety from Spain is called "Asparagus Stone". It has also been synthesised.

AXINITE (H.6.5-7) – usually found in brown, but also occurs in violet and yellow. It is acceptably hard but brittle and, therefore, is rarely cut for jewellery. A collector's stone, it may be confused with andalusite or smoky quartz.

BARYTE (H.3-3.5) – a very soft stone found in a variety of colours. Cut for collectors only.

BERYLLONITE (H.5.5) – an unimpressive, soft, colourless stone for collectors only.

BRAZILIANITE (H.5.5) – a rare pretty gem cut mainly for collectors due to its fragility. It derives its name from Brazil, where it was found. Yellow to yellowish green with a vitreous lustre.

BRONZITE – see ENSTATITE

CASSITERITE (H.6) – an ore of tin found in Cornwall and Bolivia. The reddish-brown transparent crystals are rare. It has an adamantine lustre and a high density. Cut only for collectors.

DIOPSIDE (H.5.5–6) – is found in shades of green and is usually heavily included. The most collectable variety is chrome diopside from Siberia, which is a bright emerald green; beautiful and affordable. Dark green and black varieties may show a four-rayed star and are cut en cabochon.

DIOPTASE (H.5) – a beautiful brilliant emerald green stone with strong dispersion. It is occasionally cut for collectors, but with difficulty, as it is fragile.

ENSTATITE (H.5.5) – a soft stone occurring in shades of green. The variety usually cut as a gem contains chromium making it emerald green in colour. Bronzite is a greenish brown variety and is occasionally cut for collectors, though mostly used for ornaments.

EPIDOTE (H.6.5) – a hard but fragile stone. It is strongly pleochroic (yellow, green and brown). Cut mainly for collectors. Also known as Pistacite.

HOWLITE (H.3.5) – a soft white mineral used for ornamental purposes. Its main use, once dyed, is as a simulant of turquoise.

KORNERUPINE – an unusual stone appearing green or reddish-brown depending on the way it is cut, due to its strong pleochroism. It is usually only cut for collectors. A cat's-eye variety is available. Main source is Sri Lanka.

PHENAKITE (H.7.5) – a hard but rare colourless stone cut mainly for collectors.

PISTACITE – see EPIDOTE

SCAPOLITE (H.6) – a hard but brittle stone, which is found in a wide range of colours: pink, purple, blue, yellow, grey and colourless. A violet shade is obtained by heat treatment. Also called wernerite.

SCHEELITE (H4.5-5) – a soft stone only cut for collectors. However, it is synthesised and the colourless variety has been used as a diamond simulant (not very convincingly). The coloured synthetics are used to simulate other gems.

SINHALITE (H.6.5) – an attractive yellow-brown stone found mainly in Sri Lanka. It is uncommon, but sometimes cut for collectors.

SPHALERITE (H.3.5) – a rare zinc ore. Yellowish or green in colour with a vitreous lustre. Its dispersion is 3 times higher than diamond. The crystals are only cut for collectors.

SPHENE – see TITANITE

TAAFFEITE (H.5) – extremely rare. Violet, green, pink, red or colourless. Originally found in Ireland by Count Taaffe, also found since in Sri Lanka and Tanzania.

TITANITE (H.5-5.5) – strongly pleochroic (yellow, green and brown) with a high birefringence and adamantine lustre. It is a very attractive gem but generally only cut for collectors. Also known as sphene.

WERNERITE – see SCAPOLITE

ZINCITE (H.4.5) – a unique 'gemstone', strictly speaking a synthetic, which was originally discovered growing in the smoke stack of a Polish factory. Occurs in yellow, orange, orangey-red and yellowish green. A very dense material with a high refractive index. Cut stones are very attractive although soft. It has subsequently been found in similar processing in the USA.

Buying Gemstones

TREATMENTS

Throughout the book we have discussed the many ways in which precious stones are simulated, synthesized and subjected to various treatments. Wherever possible simple identification techniques have been suggested but it must be borne in mind that even these basic methods require a certain amount of practice and experience.

Today, 90% of gemstones undergo some form of treatment and we must decide what our reaction is to this situation. How important is it to us that the beautiful gem that pleases our eye has probably been heat treated to achieve that appearance? Perhaps you take the view that we can all do with some enhancements to look our best, so why shouldn't we allow the same to be done to the ruby, sapphire or emerald that we so admire.

Before deciding it might be worth comparing some of the forms of improvement currently undertaken.

Heat and pressure treatments – these are commonly used to turn off-colour diamonds into top-colour grades. Referred to as HPHT, it is permanent and extremely difficult to detect. Fortunately, only about 1% of diamonds are suitable for this treatment. It has no known detrimental side effects.

Heat treatment – this is used on many coloured stones to improve or change their colour, mostly permanent. It may affect certain identification features of a gem, such as dichroism.

Fracture filling – this has been a common practice with emeralds for many years. They are commonly oiled to improve appearance and any fractures may be filled with glass or resins. Diamonds, rubies and certain other stones are also filled. Side effects are that the filling may be disturbed by heat during repairs to a mounting and also by ultra-sonic cleaning, leaving the stone vulnerable to cracking or breaking. It cannot be classed as permanent.

Bleaching and dyeing – this is used on several translucent and opaque gem materials, such as jade. Dyes may fade, but the process should not damage the stone.

Colour coating – a blue dye is sometimes used to improve the appearance of a yellowish diamond. This is not permanent and may be removed by wear or by nail varnish remover.

Irradiation – this was first developed at the beginning of the last century using radium; over the past twenty or thirty years it has been used to change the colour of diamonds to those not normally found in nature. They are very attractive, but the treatment is superficial, giving a surface colouration to the stone that may be lost if recut.

Laser Treatment – this is most commonly used to remove carbon inclusions in diamond and, unless the minute holes left are filled, it is possible to see them with the loupe.

Beryllium Diffusion – this latest treatment, discovered by Thai cutters, uses beryllium in conjunction with heat to enhance the colour of rubies and sapphires. It is difficult to detect.

All of the above treatments must be declared on the sales receipt or certificate and all stones thus treated should sell at a lower price than untreated stones.

Having said that, discussions among the professional bodies are on-going as to which treatments ought to be declared. The main topic is heat treatment used to improve the colour of coloured gems; due to its widespread use and its acceptance as standard practice some experts believe that, particularly for the run-of-the-mill gems, declaring such treatment is irrelevant.

SYNTHETICS AND SIMULANTS

A synthetic has to possess all the chemical features of a natural stone. In fact, it is identical to the gem that was created over millions of years under the earth.

Synthetics allow the person who cannot afford that beautiful ruby, sapphire or emerald etc., to wear one at a fraction of the price. Many people feel that, as neither they nor their friends can tell the difference anyway, they are happy to wear synthetic gems. This simply depends on your attitude to gemstones.

For me there is an indefinable romance in the genuine article; there is no romance in a synthetic or simulant. I feel that they are fine for an every-day dress-ring but that a commemoration of a special moment in one's life, such as an engagement, anniversary or the birth of a child, only the beauty formed by Mother Nature will suffice. Even if the bigger price tag means a smaller gem, it will mean more to you. You never know, it may even still carry those special mystic components in which the ancients believed.

In my opinion, simulants, things that are made to *look* like the real thing, are common and best avoided. Of course, some have a real value of their own: if you are wearing a blue spinel masquerading as a sapphire, it is still a spinel so value it as that –after all, there's a spinel in the crown jewels!

The danger in all these fakes, forgeries or imitations is that someone is going to try to sell them to you at the price of the genuine natural stone. That is why it is so important to buy from a recognised jeweller or gem merchant. Although even then genuine mistakes can be made. Look for a jeweller with recognised qualifications: FGA, Fellow of the Gemmological Association of Great Britain (now called Gem-A), the oldest and most respected qualification and also represented in the USA; or GG, Graduate Gemologist

Laser-drilled diamond. (Photo: Gem-A)

of the Gemological Institute of America. They usually display their certificates. Both Gem-A and the GIA have world-recognised test laboratories.

You will only need the services of a laboratory if you require a particularly valuable or unusual stone to be identified; usually these come with a verification certificate upon purchase. Always ask advice from a reliable source, not the seller, for the best laboratory to use. There are many reliable laboratories across the world. E.G.L. is widely represented – in the UK by Huddlestone Gemmological Consultants in Hatton Garden, London.

A reputable supplier will always issue a sales receipt stating full details of the gemstone with any treatment it has undergone. Always insist on this; if the supplier is reluctant to give these details, buy elsewhere.

A point regarding pearls. Due to the proliferation of cultured pearls over natural, the word 'cultured' in some countries is being dropped when describing pearls. This is becoming particularly prevalent in the USA, although Europe still declares authenticity.

Another point to understand is that stones are sometimes named according to their source, such as 'Kashmir Sapphire', 'Burmese Ruby', or 'Kanchan Sapphire'. These names are sometimes given by dealers to signify a colour and not its true locality; so ask!

A collector's case. (Photo: KW)

COLLECTING

Collecting gemstones as a hobby can be very rewarding and you do not have to collect top-quality stones. As in philately a thematic approach is possible: just collecting colourless stones or varieties of agate; the potential is enormous. Go to a good gem show or Hatton Garden and see for yourself. When purchasing make sure that you are told the source of the particular stone you are buying and get a receipt.

Cases to hold your gem collection are readily available from gem shows or the Gem-A shop.

Investment

There is, of course, another reason for collecting and that is for investment. This is an entirely different matter. The views on using gemstones for investment purposes are mixed, but the general consensus of opinion is that it is not the best option. As with all investment markets, the gem market is prone to fluctuation; the latest high was in the 1980s, overall, the market has dropped. The present worldwide economic situation has given a boost to investment in gems (and gold), therefore prices of investment stones are on the increase.

If you are keen to make an investment, where you buy becomes of even more importance. The internet, although it proliferates with sites offering stones for sale, is best avoided in this case.

You must ensure that the gems you are buying for your portfolio are of the best colour, clarity and quality that you can afford. They should only be bought from a reliable source, preferably from your own country under the advice of a qualified gemmologist. Beware: there are a lot of investment scams about. Gem Shows should not be relied on: a stand at a gem show is no guarantee of reputation.

Coloured stones or fancies, as they are often termed, call for a slightly different method of judgement, the four 'Cs' still apply but in differing priority.

Colour, that is depth and purity of colour, counts for approximately 50% of the value of the gem, clarity for 25-30%, cut is next, but carat weight comes last. Gemstones for investment are the big four: diamond (coloured), ruby, sapphire and emerald. There are a few other stones worthy of consideration but they are not as reliable, as new sources and fashion can affect the market.

Any of the many Gemmological Institutes around the world will offer advice but bear in mind, this sort of investment is for the very rich.

The best advice is to buy for beauty and enjoyment, buy for quality in preference to size and only buy untreated stones. If they increase in value above inflation then that is a bonus.

Always inspect stones in both daylight and artificial light, they should look as good in both.

Remember that total carat weight refers to the weight of all the stones in a piece of jewellery. If, for example, a ring is said to have a total carat weight of 50 points – or half a carat – and contains ten stones then, on average, each stone would only weigh 5 points: very small and individually of low value compared to single stone of 50 points.

JEWELLERY

Although this book is primarily about gemstones, perhaps a few notes about the precious metals used in jewellery will not go amiss. However, to put values in to context, taking the average engagement ring, the gemstone constitutes 75-90% of the value.

Gold – pure gold is 24 karat but is generally alloyed with other metals to produce a range of coloured golds. For instance to achieve red, yellow or green the gold is alloyed with varying proportions of silver, copper or tin. White gold is an alloy with nickel, palladium and zinc. All these mixes reduce the eventual gold content to 75% or 18 karat. If 14 karat gold is acceptable the shade of colour is wider. The lowest purity of gold accepted in the UK is 9 karat. White gold is sometimes rhodium-plated to make it more reflective and mask solder joints.

Palladium – of the platinum family, discovered in 1803, this is sometimes used as a cheaper alternative to platinum. Its density is nearly half that of platinum. It is occasionally used as an alloy to produce a good quality white gold. It is found associated with platinum in Russia, Australia and the USA and with copper nickel deposits in South Africa and the USA.

Pinchbeck – is an alloy of 83% copper and 17% zinc, with a remarkable resemblance to gold, though much lighter. Now found only in antique jewellery, pinchbeck was introduced at the beginning of the 18th century.

Platinum – thirty times rarer than gold, platinum is the purest metal used in jewellery: ninety-five per cent pure, hence the 950 hallmark. Due to its purity, it is hypoallergenic. Known since ancient times, it only came into its own in the early 1900s; the discovery in 1924 of the world's largest deposit near Johannesburg secured its future. It became popular for use in jewellery at the beginning of the 20th century due to its resistance to tarnishing.

A new innovation is platinum plating on silver, which provides a hard-wearing, non-tarnishing finish at reasonable cost.

Rolled Gold – was developed in 1817 and consists of a thin sheet of gold bonded to a sheet of base metal using a method similar to that used for producing Sheffield Plate.

Silver – sterling silver is 92.5 % silver. Brittania silver is 95% but is little used today. Silver is often rhodium plated to prevent tarnishing. The purity of European silver has varied widely over the years unlike the UK standards.

Hallmark on a silver pocket fruit knife. The series of stamps showing, from left to right, the Sheffield Assay Office, the lion passant, the year mark (1898-99), and the maker's mark (unknown). (Photo: KW)

HALLMARKS

A hallmarking system has been in use in the UK with little change for hundreds of years. In 1972 the UK became a signatory to the International Convention on Hallmarks, alongside Austria, the Czech Republic, Denmark, Finland, Eire, Netherlands, Norway, Portugal, Sweden and Switzerland. This means that a convention hallmark

Convention symbols

| Gold | Silver | Platinum |

Compulsory symbols

Sponsor's or maker's mark   *Metal and fineness (purity) mark*   *Assay Office Mark*

Voluntary symbols

Traditional fineness mark   *Date mark*

struck by the UK Assay Offices will be recognised by all members of the Convention. Conversely the same mark on precious metals by other Convention members will be recognised in the UK as indicating that the item is of the required standard of purity. European countries that are

not members include Spain, Belgium, France, Italy, Germany, Greece and Luxembourg, some of which are expected to join in the near future.

According to the UK Hallmarking Act in 1999, only three of the previous five marks are now compulsory: the maker's mark, the purity mark and the assay office mark. The traditional fineness mark and date letter are no longer obligatory. There are four assay offices in the UK – London, Birmingham, Sheffield and Edinburgh. For further information on hallmarking approach should be made to: The British Hallmarking Council, PO Box 18133, London EC2V 8JY.

In Arab countries it is traditional for women to collect gold as their security, so purity of gold is of prime importance. Hence all jewellery carries a purity mark for 18 or 22 carat gold.

The Genuine Article

Buying antique jewellery is no guarantee of gems being genuine, fakes have been around for a long, long time – the gemstone in that Victorian ring may not be all it seems to be! And, of course, it is a lucrative business to fake antiques themselves.

This was particularly prevalent just after the second world war when the jewellery industry was going through a very hard time. Purchase tax of up to 125% had been put on luxury items, including all new jewellery, but antique items were exempt. Consequently many jewellery workshops began to produce 'antique' jewels, mostly Victorian in style, and sell them to antique dealers. This practice lasted from 1947 through to the late 'fifties. It was highly illegal but a way for the struggling industry to survive. The materials used tended to be genuine: precious metals of hallmarking standard (but, of course, not hallmarked so as not to give the game away) and real gems were used. The stones were carefully chosen to match the period being copied. So the buyer was getting his money's worth, just not the history. No one knows how many of these replicas are still around and probably never will.

Gemstones around the World

On holiday or on a business trip we often consider bringing home a nice gift for the husband or wife. Time is sometimes short and, in the rush to pick the right gift or memento for ourselves, we might not be as thorough as we ought in checking what we are buying and are most likely to fall prey to a con. It is critical to plan early in the trip and decide the sort of item you want, be it a gemstone or a piece of jewellery.

So the next few pages are designed to give a little help on where to buy and what to avoid. Obviously, many countries have reliable jewellers who can provide many gems either set or unset, so it is unnecessary to list these. Instead, unusual items that may be found locally are described. It is impossible to cover every country in the world so I have grouped them loosely into continents.

AFRICA
North Africa – Common in the souks of Tunisia are amber necklaces made of fake or compressed amber impregnated with amber perfume. The amber used in perfumes comes from whales' ambergris and is nothing to do with fossil amber. Silver here is not to be recommended, being low grade. The best red coral is fished along the shores of Algeria & Tunisia but generally sent to Italy for working. Strict controls apply to collecting and exporting.

West Africa – Several West African countries, including Angola, the Congo, Sierra Leone and Liberia, are in states of political unrest. The Rebels trade rough diamonds to buy armaments. Approximately 4% per annum of diamond rough is smuggled out. In May 2000 South Africa led a group of 40 Governments to set up the Kimberley Process. This involved a certification procedure for all rough diamonds crossing international borders. Unfortunately once the stones have been smuggled out into the hands of the unscrupulous dealers and faceted they are impossible to identify. These are known as 'Conflict Diamonds'.

Madagascar (formerly the Malagasy Republic) – With the discovery of sapphires in 1998, Madagascar became a major producer of high-quality gems, rivalling Sri Lanka. Lines of gem dealer's shops have appeared in the towns, where once there was little of interest. A wide range of precious stones have now been found on the island. Sapphires, garnets, chalcedony, chrysoberyl, iolite, emerald, kunzite, ruby, topaz, tourmaline and zircon. Many of these are exported to Thailand for cutting and marketing.

Unfortunately the infrastructure lags behind the enormous potential of the recent discoveries, but investment is now being received to improve the primitive nature of the mining. Gem-A has now set up training courses in French using approved tutors, so that local students can sit the usual diploma examinations.

CENTRAL & SOUTH AMERICA
Brazil – A visit to Rio de Janeiro is the highlight to any trip to South America. Brazil supplies the world with an enormous range of different gemstone from amethyst to tourmaline. Possibly the two most important gems are diamond and emerald, but it also provides a rich supply of topaz. Also, the best alexandrite outside Russia is found here.

Diamond was originally discovered in 1725 and soon began to flood the market. Emerald was discovered much later. The many shops in Rio and São Paulo have superb displays of the many types of gemstones. Unfortunately as in so many of the gem cities of the world, crime is always a problem. Awareness is of paramount importance in these areas and it is important to buy only from reputable jewellers.

As well as selling gems, "Realgems" in Rio runs gemmology courses and has a well-equipped laboratory. To the south of the country is Rio Grande Do Sul, which is a wonderful source of geodes and crystal clusters. These are on ready sale in the local tourist shops

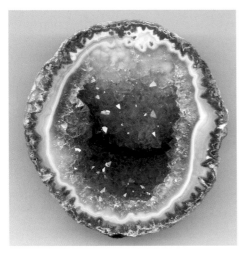

Amethyst Geode. (Photo: KW)

Larimar (Photo: KW)

Chile – A few gems of interest are here: lapis lazuli is available but the quality is variable, having calcite veins running through and often lacking the pyrites that makes the Afghan variety so attractive. Chrysocolla and turquoise are also found.

Colombia – Although not a popular holiday location, it would be wrong to exclude it as it provides the world's finest emeralds. The mines operate erratically due to the influence of the criminal element and the supply of the gem is inconsistent. This has had an effect on the market for natural emerald, allowing the excellent synthetics to take a larger market share.

Dominican Republic – An increasingly popular holiday spot. It has a fascinating secret: a supply of amber. Not, however, the amber we are used to seeing, but a tropical variety. It is found in what is now called the 'Amber Valley' and, instead of bees and flies as inclusions, tropical insects are found, even small lizards. It is worth looking out for.

Another unusual gem is larimar, a sky-blue translucent-to-opaque stone with white cloud-like markings. It is also known as Atlantis Stone with a hardness between 5 and 7 on the Mohs scale. It is cut *en cabochon*.

Mexico – This country is famous for the fire opal but other opals are also found there. An opal with a tan body is sold, which is often smoked to enhance the tan colour and thereby increase the fire of the stone. A test for this is to wet the stone with saliva, this will reduce the fire, which will return on drying. Water opal is also offered.

Carved jadeite is also marketed but probably sourced from South America.

West Indies – In certain countries, particularly Jamaica, Trinidad and Tobago, cases have been reported of illicit dealing in black coral. The export of black coral is strictly forbidden and if found by Customs will lead to confiscation and heavy fines.

NORTH AMERICA

Canada – There are many excellent jewellers in the major cities so buying isn't a problem. Canada is now a frontrunner in the mining of high-quality diamonds. The major 'Ekati' mine is situated 125 miles south of the Arctic Circle. The cut stones are identified by the 'Canadamark' laser engraved on the girdle.

Other new finds are being made in Canada. Emerald deposits have been discovered in the Yukon and 'true blue' beryl has also been found. The latter is heavily included and similar to emerald; availability is uncertain at present.

Several gemstones are found in the Rocky Mountains. Among the peaks behind Mount Princeton, large crystals of aquamarine may be seen in the veins of granite and smoky quartz. Walking along some stretches of the divide and rivers, quartz, garnet, agate, amethyst and turquoise may be picked up. Ammolite and mammoth ivory are also offered here.

United States of America – It is impossible in a book this size to try and describe what to find and where to look in such a massive country. There are some excellent guides produced locally.

A good place to see what is available is at the Annual Intergem Tucson Show usually held in February. Over 4000 exhibitors from all over the world exhibit the latest gems and minerals, from small to large; some items for sale require a forklift and truck to get them home!

But even here one needs to be aware. The Trade Descriptions Act we have in the UK does not apply in the USA and they do not have an equivalent.

The USA is the biggest gemstone market in the world. The Gemological Institute of America is the second oldest institute and its laboratories are second to none. GIA diamond certification is accepted worldwide.

The Smithsonian Museum in Washington has one of the finest collections of gemstones and this is where to see the Hope diamond.

Hong Kong (Photo: KW)

ASIA

Hong Kong – A trading centre for everything: a shopper's paradise. Naturally there are many jeweller's shops and several gemmologists display their certificates. Hong Kong is not a producer of gemstones but has an impressive display in the large shopping centres. It is an important diamond market.

Gold sales are different here as the dealers quote in the Tael, which is 37.429 grams as opposed to the Troy ounce of 32 grams. Buying from street vendors is as inadvisable here as anywhere else. There is a lot of dyed jade offered to the unsuspecting.

India – India was the historic provider of many of the most famous gems of today. The ancient diamonds engraved with religious inscriptions were highly prized by the Princes and Maharajahs. Both the Koh-I-Nor, discovered around Hyderabad in 1304, and The Great Mogul diamonds were from India.

Emeralds, although mentioned in Indian history, were not in fact discovered in the country until the early 1940s.

India today has an active diamond cutting industry, with a few stones still being mined in the north of the country. The range of gems apart from diamond is quite wide and they are readily available. Only deal with recognised dealers and do not buy off the street.

Myanmar (formerly Burma) – Due to the political situation and the imposition of economic sanctions (the import of gemstones from Myanmar is banned by the United States), Myanmar is not a popular place to go on holiday.

Myanmar historically has been one of the great sources of gemstones. The rubies particularly are held in the highest esteem. They will, however, still be available to accredited buyers at the state-run Myanmar Gem Enterprise auctions that are held in Rangoon. Most of their best gems now go to India and Thailand.

Pakistan – Pakistan has a wide range of gems available; only buy from recognised dealers, do not buy off the street.

Singapore – Jewellery shops abound, so pick a recommended one. The Singapore Gem factory is a tourist attraction where gem cutting and polishing may be witnessed. The Tael unit of weight is also used.

Operculum cat's eyes are found around the shores of the islands.

Sri Lanka – The 'land of gems', just about every gemstone except diamond and precious opal is found in Sri Lanka. The 'City Of Gems' is Ratnapura to the east of Colombo, where many gemshops are to be found. Because this is the 'City of Gems' it does not mean that you can take everything at face value. Street sellers have synthetics and simulants mixed up with some indifferent natural stones, so, as always, only buy from recognised outlets. There are Government-approved shops but their prices are generally high so you're unlikely to find a bargain. Museums displaying many of the precious stones found on the island are a good starting point to get used to seeing the different varieties and what they look like.

Thailand – Probably the largest gem centre in the Far East. Bangkok is a thriving city with gemstone supermarkets, which are well organised and offer a dazzling display of stones. Certification is also possible on the premises, but remember the advice given under 'Buying Gemstones'.

The gemstones offered come from Thailand itself as well as from other countries, such as Sri Lanka, Myanmar (Burma), India and Madagascar.

Chantaburi, about 150 miles from Bangkok, is the major trading centre for the sapphires and rubies found locally around Khao Ploei Waen, the gem mountain. The vast majority of the rubies and sapphires are heat treated to improve their colour. It was here that the Thai craftsmen developed the latest technique of beryllium diffusion.

At weekends the gem market located in the centre of the old town is a thriving mass of dealers from all round

Gem dealers at Ratnapura. The buyers are qualified gemmologists, the amateur should avoid buying this way. (Photo: CW)

the Far East. This market is for the professional so it is better to do your buying in the Bangkok supermarket.

A word of warning: scams are very common and the unscrupulous prey on the unsuspecting tourist. A casual meeting with a local 'businessman' who offers an apparently good source of jewellery tax free or at a special tourist rate is a common set-up. You will be sold possibly genuine goods but of inferior quality and worth less than half what you paid for them. These con artists are very convincing, so do not be caught. Many have been.

AUSTRALASIA

Australia – Home of the opal (the national stone), Australia also produces huge quantities of diamond, though mainly industrial. Sapphire is also mined.

Of course, you can buy all these in the jeweller's shops in Sydney, Melbourne, Canberra or any of the large cities, but if you want to see opals and sapphires in their natural state, you need to go to the mining areas. Unfortunately some of these are pretty remote although some tours do include visits.

Opal is mined in Queensland, New South Wales, South and Western Australia. Perhaps the most famous mining area is Coober Pedy, the aboriginal name meaning "white man in a hole". Which is in fact how many of the miners live.

There is an amazing variety of opals on offer: black, white and precious as well as an unusual selection of opalised wood and polished ironstone with opal inclusions, well worth considering for pendants. Avoid buying opals displayed in water.

The main mining centre for sapphires is Inverell, New South Wales. Visitors can visit the Mining Museum and even 'fossick' for gems themselves. Apart from blue (not always dark, as rumoured), a wide range of colours is found, including yellow, green, red, orange and pink as well as bicoloured. The output has dropped over the past few years and much has been bought by Thailand

Mookite Necklace. (Photo MM)

to be sold on as coming from other sources.

Emeralds are also found, though not in commercial quantity and generally of low quality. Good-quality chrysoprase is mined, the total output being sent to Hong Kong for processing and sale.

Australia also has the highest output of top-quality nephrite jade in the world. Geodes (hollow spheres) and thundereggs (also round but the middle is solid, filled with agate or quartz) are found in New South Wales and Queensland; they are on sale in the collectors' shops.

Another material used for beads and cabochons is a variety of jasper called Mookite. It occurs in a wide variety of earthy shades.

New Zealand – Nephrite jade, soapstone, garnet, bowenite and paua shell are all found in New Zealand. The Maoris carve jade and soapstone. Kauri gum, a copal resin, is also found here and may be mistaken for amber.

EUROPE

Belgium – Antwerp rivals Amsterdam in its handling of diamonds. Fifty per cent of rough diamonds pass through the city. The Diamond District near the railway station is a vast cluster of dealer's shops. The Diamond Market is where traders buy not only diamonds but also a wide range of precious stones.

The large Diamond Museum houses a priceless collection covering the history of this favourite of all gemstones.

Eire – County Galway is the source of Connemara Marble, which can be confused with jade. Jewellery is produced locally. Kilkenny Marble is black and contains numerous fossils; as well as its major use in churches, it is used to make rosary beads.

France – The Auvergne region is volcanic and consequently heavily mineralised. It is not unusual to see the sale of local minerals in lay-bys along the sides of the roads. Among the local specimens you may find amethyst, rock crystal, fluorspar, sapphire, ruby, aquamarine, emerald, peridot and zircon. These will not be of gem quality but good as shelf objects or talking points.

France has several lapidary museums, such as those in Avignon, Perigueux and Castlenay Castle. Of particular interest is the diamond museum in St Claude in the Jura. This has a good display of gemstones both natural and synthetic. The equipment used for the manufacture of the synthetic diamonds is also shown together with the tools used for diamond cutting. The work done in the associated workshops supplies the clock and watch industry in nearby Switzerland. A video is available describing the various processes.

The local area also produces excellent briar trees used for pipe making and a museum of pipes and their history is adjacent.

Germany – The place not to miss is Idar Oberstein, the gem centre of this country. The magnificent Edelstein museum of gemstones is enough to take your breath away. If you want to see what real gems look like, then this is the place to visit. Not far away are the traditional cutting mills where you can see agate being worked on giant grindstones; the variety of agates is fascinating. There is a wealth of gem and jewellery shops in the town: Ruppenthals is well worth a visit as is the Schmuck und Mineralien Haus [Jewellery and Mineral House] in Wasserschieder Strasse.

An important gem and mineral show is held in the Munich Trade Centre each Autumn.

Italy – If you are near Naples, the centre for coral working is at Torre del Greco, which is also the biggest jewellery manufacturing area, including cameo carving. Cameos are carved from coral, agate and shell; quality varies so go for the best you can afford.

Agate cutter at Idar Oberstein. (Photo: KW)

Netherlands – If you are flying into Schiphol Airport at Amsterdam, you can buy your diamonds *in situ* while you are waiting for you next flight!

Amsterdam is one of the biggest diamond cutting centres in the world. The factories of Stoeltie Diamonds and Gassan Diamonds offer guided tours where cutting may be seen. The Amsterdam Diamond Centre is also open to the public. Stones can be purchased at all these places.

Russia – The most famous gem from Russia is of course alexandrite, but·this is becoming increasing rare from this source. Most gems on offer are the opaque materials such as malachite, charoite, serpentine (known as Zmeevik), jasper, rhodonite, amazonite, nephrite, agate and dolerite. These are found mostly in the form of ornaments, boxes and occasionally as cabochons in jewellery. Be warned: Russia is a major supplier of synthetics.

Spain – Andalusia first gave the world that beautiful pleochroic gemstone Andalusite. Although today it is mainly sourced from Brazil, you may still find some on sale in Cordoba, which is a good centre of jewellery with a jewellery museum, the Museo de Joyeria Regina.

There are mineralogical museums in Valverde de Camino and Seville.

Andalusite's associated mineral chiastolite is found in Northern Spain and is particularly treasured in this strongly religious area due to the cross formed in the stone.

Amethyst is very popular and is in plentiful supply.

Majorica simulated pearls are produced on the island of **Majorca** and are an extremely good and popular souvenir. They should not be confused with cultured pearls, though they are difficult to distinguish.

Peridot is prevalent throughout the **Canary Islands**. The gem variety of the olivine found in the basalt lava around the area, it is easy to pick up pieces of the black rock and see the olive green crystal within. Peridot jewellery is found in many of the local shops. Quality varies so ensure you buy only the best colour and exclude the pale stones.

Switzerland – Geneva is a major centre for the sale of precious gems. Auctions of some of the world's finest jewellery are held there: the Duchess of Windsor's collection was sold for millions of pounds a few years ago. One of the best gemmological testing laboratories, the Gubelin, is based in Lucerne.

There are certainly many jewellers in Switzerland and the same comments go for buying there as most places; however prices do tend to be higher.

Turkey – Probably the best-known mineral to come from this country is Meerschaum, long used for bowls of tobacco pipes and cigarette holders. They are beautifully carved and antique examples command high prices.

A gem that has recently entered the market place is diaspore, a pretty pleochroic stone similar in its coloration to andalusite.

United Kingdom – The major centres for jewellery and gemstones are London and Birmingham. However, there are many excellent and reliable jewellers in the major cities. Pick a shop with trained staff, certificates are usually on show.

There are extremely few gemstones actually found in the UK and even those are not of gem quality. There are, however, some organics: amber from North Yorkshire, jet from Whitby, Blue John, together with other fluorspars, and Jasper from the Peak District, Slate (though not normally thought of as material for jewellery, it can be attractive) may be found in the factory shops of North Wales. There are also still two gold mines in Wales: one near Llandovery and the other near Dolgellau, where jewellery may be purchased containing approximately 10% of the local gold.

Smoky or brown quartz was sourced in the Cairngorm Mountains of Scotland but is nearly exhausted. It was used extensively in Celtic jewellery, which now uses heat-treated amethyst imported from Brazil as a simulant. Iona Stone, a form of serpentine, found in the Hebrides is used locally in the making of jewellery. An excellent gem and rock museum is situated in Creetown, Newton Stewart.

Cornwall is a highly mineralised area and although amethyst, smoky quartz and turquoise have been found in the china clay pits it is sold only as mineral specimens. Some fine serpentine material is found around the Lizard and is carved in to a wide variety of jewellery and ornaments. Camborne has an excellent Museum of Mining and Minerals.

THE MIDDLE-EAST

Gold is held in high esteem in all Arab countries and the quality in terms of karatage is very important. That is why most gold on sale is either 18 or 22 karat. This is sold by the gram. There are 32 grams to the Troy ounce (not the 28 grams to the ounce as in domestic cooking). Gold is always sold in this way. The small tola bars are sold in troy ounce sizes.

When you visit the gold souks in **Saudi Arabia**, **Kuwait**, **Bahrain**, **Dubai** and **Qatar** you will be amazed at the quantity of it on display. Some of it will be unlike anything you have seen before. Much of it provides the necessary items that the bridegroom has to buy, by tradition, to give to his bride as a dowry. There will also be other items more suitable for western wear.

When you decide to buy, the first thing to do is to ask the price per gram, as this varies from day to day. Then, when you have selected the piece you want, it is weighed and you are given the price for the piece.

A point to watch: avoid buying jewellery containing many 'gemstones', these are generally not very good quality, possibly glass or paste and are also included in the weight of the item. Don't pay a gold price for glass!

The gold is good. Silver tends not to be so good; it is usually not of Sterling quality and can be considerably lower. It is best avoided. An exception is if you visit the **Oman**. Here the silver Maria Theresa Taler has been accepted as a trading token by the hill tribesmen for hundreds of years and they will not accept anything else. The Thaler, originally minted in Austria, is still being minted in several countries today; it always carries a date of 1780, regardless of when it was actually produced. They are readily available around the souks of Muttrah. They are not sterling silver (925) but 833 fine containing 0.752 oz.

Bahrain and **Dubai** were once the major pearling centres around the Arabian Gulf. The production of pearls has now dropped considerably, due to the influx of cultured pearls and to pollution, it is still possible to find a few dealers around. Dubai has a very interesting museum showing pearling in days gone by.

Turquoise, mostly veined, is found around Medina together with chalcedony and is used in the local jewellery.

'Saudi diamonds' are found in the deserts around Riyadh

Gold souk in Kuwait. (Photo: KW)

Maria Theresa Taler. (Photo: KW)

Gypsum 'sand rose'

and are, in fact, quartz pebbles. They were collected by the ex-pats and sent off for cutting and polishing as souvenirs. Another local oddity is the 'Sand Rose' found in the deserts. This is gypsum that has formed into interlocking plate-like crystals. These are readily available for a modest price in the souks. They come in a wide range of sizes, from a few inches across to a foot or more.

Uncut 'Saudi diamond'

Israel – Next only to Antwerp in importance to diamond trading, it is also a major cutting centre. Ramat Gan is the hub of this business housing both the Israeli Diamond and Coloured Stone Exchanges.

Israel's national stone is the Eilat named after the popular port and coastal resort on the shores of the Gulf of Aqaba. Reputedly found in the legendary mines of King Solomon, which are a few miles away, it is used *en cabochon* for pendants, rings and earrings, set in gold or silver. Usually green, and similar to malachite, it has a wide range of shades and markings.

This now brings our trip around the world to a close. It is not possible to list all the wonderful rarities and oddities, but it is hoped that it has aroused a sense of awareness of what is out there and how to go about adding it to your own personal collection.

Gems on the Internet

There are literally hundreds of websites on the Internet dealing with gems. Most of them are offering a wide range for sale in the form of loose stones or set in jewellery. These may be explored at leisure but bear in mind there are risks involved in purchasing from these sources as you don't see what you are buying until you have paid.

However, there are several useful and informative sites and some of these are listed below:

www.gem-a.info
GEM-A, The Gemmological Association of Great Britain. Details of membership, instrument sales, books etc. Gem-A provides in-house and correspondence courses for its prestigious FGA and DGA qualifications in gemmology.

www.giagem.org
G.I.A. (USA) – Details of membership, instrument sales, books and educational facilities.

www.gem.org.au
Gemmological Association of Australia – Gallery of Australian Gems.

www.cigem.ca
Canadian Institute of Gemmology.

www.gemstone.org
International Coloured Gemstone Association – Excellent database of gemstone information.

www.nhm.ac.uk
Natural History Museum – London home of the national gemstone collection.

www.nmnh.si.edu/minsci
Smithsonian Institute – Visit here to see the Hope diamond, amongst others.

www.multicolour.com
Multicolour – An American company selling gemstones. Their catalogue serves as a very good database of illustrations and properties.

www.atggems.com
All That Glitters – An American dealer in coloured gemstones.

www.chatham.com
Chatham Created Gems – Read the story of Chatham synthetic diamonds, emeralds etc.

www.edelsteinmuseum.de
Idar Oberstein – Information on the famous gem museum.

www.gemesis.com
Gemesis Diamonds – A major manufacturer of synthetic diamonds.

www.debeersgroup.com
De Beers – Home page of the biggest and oldest diamond dealer.

www.gemrock.net
Creetown Museum – A UK website in South-West Scotland. Plenty of useful information.

www.holtsgems.co.uk
R. Holt Ltd. – Based in Hatton Garden, this is one of the largest gem dealers in the UK. Also runs a school of gemmology and jewellery.

www.ebay.co.uk and **www.ebay.com**
A wide range of gems and jewellery are offered on the various ebay sites, thousands in fact. Even though many of the items being auctioned are genuine and at attractive prices, particular care is needed when buying. Remember 'genuine' is not necessarily natural, synthetics are sometimes described as genuine. And if a seller has lied about a so-called gem, it may be difficult to recover your 'lost' money. "Buyer beware!"

Appendix 1 – Glossary

Adularescence	Name given to the 'opalescence' seen in moonstone.
Alluvial	Deposit of gem materials in dried up riverbeds.
Asterism	The feature shown in star stones i.e. Ruby and Sapphire.
Birefringence	The difference between the refractive indices of a doubly refractive stone.
Conflict diamonds	Illegal stones smuggled out of countries where mining is done by slave labour or in the control of criminal organisations. All reputable dealers outlaw trading in these diamonds.
Cat's eye	An effect exhibited by some gems where fine fibrous inclusions cause a changeable band of light to appear and to move across a cabochon-cut stone. Known as 'chatoyancy', this is often seen in quartz, chrysoberyl and tourmaline.
Cleavage	The tendency of crystals to break along certain definite directions producing more or less smooth surfaces. This is a feature used particularly in the cutting of large diamonds.
Density	See **specific gravity**.
Dichroism	An effect seen in some doubly refractive gems where a stone appears as different colours when viewed from different directions.
Dichroscope	Instrument used to study dichroism.
Dispersion	A property of gems generally referred to as it's 'fire'.
Enhancement	Any process that artificially improves the appearance of a gemstone i.e. heat treatment, laser drilling to remove inclusions, dyeing etc.
Fisheye	Particularly applied to diamonds, this refers to a shallow cut stone that exhibits a white circle when viewed through the table.
Fluorescence	A property shown by some minerals and gems to glow when exposed to ultra-violet light.
Heavy liquids	Liquids used by gemmologists for checking the specific gravity of gemstones. They are all corrosive or poisonous.
Inclusion	Any foreign body or cavity within the body of a stone. Often used by gemmologists to aid identification of the gem.

Intaglio	A gem with an engraved design.
Irradiation	A radioactive treatment to improve or change the colour of a gem.
Lustre	The surface appearance of a polished gemstone i.e. quartz – glassy, diamond – adamantine, turquoise – waxy. Also the orient of pearl.
Matrix	The base rock enclosing a crystal or mineral.
Pleochroism	As dichroism but displaying more than two colours.
Polariscope	An instrument used, among other things, to inspect gems to indicate single or double refraction.
Polymorph	Gem of the same chemical composition but crystallising in more than one crystal form.
Refraction	The specific angle at which light bends when passing through a gem, which is measured and interpreted into the *refractive index* for that stone. Double refraction means that the stone splits the light ray into two and each ray has a different angle so the stone has two refractive indices. Gemmologists use a refractometer to establish the refractive index of a gem.
Simulant	Any stone that is purported to be another type of stone without having any of its chemical properties. (cf. **synthetic**)
Specific Gravity	The S.G. (specific gravity) of a gemstone refers to its weight in air compared to the weight of an equal volume of water. Therefore, the higher the S.G. of a stone the heavier it will weigh compared to gems of a lower S.G. Consequently a one carat diamond (S.G. 3.51) is smaller in size than a one carat tourmaline (S.G. 3.00) because the diamond is denser than the tourmaline. So, the higher the S.G. the smaller the stone of an equivalent weight.
Spectroscope	An instrument used to view the spectrum of a gem in order to assist in its identification. A rainbow of colours forming the spectrum is crossed by a series of black vertical lines signifying various chemicals in its makeup.
Star Stone	A stone that exhibits a star effect or 'asterism' as described in the section on ruby.
Synthetic	A laboratory-made gem that is, to all intents and purposes, chemically identical to the natural stone. (cf. **simulant**)
Zoning	Colour banding that occurs in natural and synthetic gemstones. The banding is generally straight or angular in the natural gem, but curved in the synthetic

Appendix 2 – Rainbow of Colours

Colour	Gemstone
Red/Pink	Almandine Garnet
	Amber
	Beryl
	Coral
	Danburite
	Diamond
	Fire opal
	Fluorspar
	Kunzite
	Morganite
	Pyrope Garnet
	Rhodochrosite
	Rhodolite Garnet
	Rhodonite
	Rose Quartz
	Rubellite (Tourmaline)
	Ruby
	Sapphire
	Spinel
	Topaz
	Zircon
Orange	Amber
	Hessonite Garnet
	Fire opal
	Sapphire (Padparadsha)
Yellow	Amber
	Beryl (Heliodor)
	Chrysoberyl
	Citrine
	Danburite
	Diamond
	Fluorspar
	Jadeite
	Spinel (very rare)
	Topaz
	Tourmaline
	Zircon
Brown	Amber
	Andalusite
	Beryl
	Cairngorm
	Diamond
	Fluorspar
	Hessonite Garnet
	Jadeite
	Obsidian
	Peridot

Colour	Gemstone
	Quartz (Smoky)
	Tourmaline
	Zircon
Green	Andalusite
	Emerald
	Beryl
	Chrome Chalcedony
	Chrysoberyl
	Chrysocolla
	Demantoid Garnet
	Fluorspar
	Grossular Garnet
	Hiddenite
	Jadeite
	Malachite
	Nephrite
	Peridot
	Sapphire
	Spinel (rare)
	Tourmaline
	Zircon
Blue	Aquamarine
	Benitoite
	Diamond
	Fluorspar
	Iolite
	Jadeite
	Lapis Lazuli
	Sapphire
	Sodalite
	Spinel
	Tanzanite
	Topaz
	Tourmaline (Indicolite)
	Turquoise
	Zircon
Violet	Almandine Garnet
	Amethyst
	Fluorspar
	Jadeite
	Kunzite
	Sapphire
	Tanzanite
	Tourmaline
	Zircon

The above shows only some of the range of colours of the gems covered in the book.

Appendix 3 – Specific Gravity & Refractive Index of Gemstones

Gemstone	Specific Gravity	Refractive Index
Water	*1.00*	*1.333*
Alexandrite	3.72	1.742-1.759
Amber	1.03-1.10	1.54
Andalusite	3.15	1.633-1.644
Apatite	3.15-3.22	1.63-1.65
Aquamarine	2.69	1.570-1.586
Benitoite	3.64	1.757-1.804
Beryl – Morganite	2.80	1.58-1.60
– Heliodor	2.69	1.58-1.60
Chrysoberyl	3.72	1.742-1.757
Chrysocolla	2.1-2.20	1.50
Coral	2.68	1.630-1.636
Corundum - Synthetic	4.00	1.76-1.77
Cubic Zirconia (CZ)	5.56-6.00	2.17
Danburite	3.00	1.630-1.636
Diaspore	3.3-3.5	1.70-1.75
Diamond	*3.52*	*2.417-2.420*
Emerald – Natural	2.71	1.585-1.593
– Synthetic	2.66-2.71	1.56-1.563
Fire Opal	2.00	1.453-1.455
Fluorspar	3.17-3.19	1.43
Garnet – Almandine	3.97	1.75-1.82
– Demantoid	3.84	1.88-1.89
– Hessonite	3.65	1.742-1.748
– Pyrope	3.75	1.74-1.75
Glass	2.00-6.00	1.44-1.90
Hematite	4.9-5.3	2.94-3.22
Hiddenite	3.17-3.23	1.660-1.659
Iolite	2.57-2.66	1.53-1.55
Ivory – Dentine	1.85	1.54
– Vegetable	1.40	1.54
Jadeite	3.3-3.5	1.65-1.68
Jet	1.10-1.40	1.64-1.68
Kunzite	3.17-3.23	1.660-1.679
Kyanite	3.17-3.23	1.716-1.731
Labradorite	2.70-2.72	1.56-1.57

Gemstone		Specific Gravity	Refractive Index
Lapis Lazuli		2.80	1.50
Malachite		3.74-3.95	1.65-1.90
Moissanite (synthetic)		3.22	2.65-2.69
Moonstone		2.57	1.52-1.54
Nephrite Jade		2.9-3.02	1.60-1.65
Obsidian		2.40	1.5
Opal		2.10	1.44-1.47
Pearl	– Natural	2.71	–
	– Cultured	2.75	–
Pcridot		3.34	1.654 1.689
Quartz		2.65	1.544-1.553
Rhodochrosite		3.45-3.70	1.597-1.817
Rhodonite		3.5-3.7	1.71-1.73
Ruby		3.99	1.759-1.779
Sapphire		3.99	1.759-1.779
Sillimanite		3.25	1.658-1.677
Sodalite		2.2-2.4	1.48
Spinel	– Natural	3.60	1.714-1.736
	– Synthetic	3.63	1.725-1.728
Sunstone		2.62-2.65	1.54-1.55
Tanzanite		3.35	1.692-1.700
Topaz		3.53-3.56	1.607-1.637
Tortoiseshell		1.29	1.55-1.56
Tourmaline		3.05	1.616-1.652
Turquoise		2.60-2.80	1.61-1.65
YAG		4.58	1.834
Zircon (Normal)		4.4-4.69	1.92-1.993

Appendix 4 – Translations

English	German	French	Italian	Spanish
agate	Achat	agate	agata	ágata
amber	Bernstein	ambre	ambra	ámbar
amethyst	Amethyst	améthyste	ametista	amatista
aquamarine	Aquamarin	aigue-marine	acquamarina	aguamarina
beryl	Beryll	béryl	berillo	berilo
black	schwarz	noir	nero	negro
bloodstone (heliotrope)	Heliotrop	sanguine	eliotropio	sanguina
blue	blau	bleu	blu/azzurro	azul
carat	Karat	carat	carato	quilate
coral	Koralle	corail	corallo	coral
cornelian	Karneol	cornaline	carniola	cornalina
corundum	Korund	corindon	corobino	corindon
diamond	Diamant	diamant	diamante	diamante
emerald	Smaragd	émeraude	smeraldo	esmeralda
enamel	Emaille	émail	smalto	esmalte
garnet	Granat	grenat	granato	granate
glass	Glas	verre	vetro	vidrio
gold	Gold	or	oro	oro
green	grun	vert	verde	verde
ivory	Elfenbein	ivoire/rohart/marfil	avorio	marfil
jade	Jade	jade	giada	jade
jasper	Jaspis	jaspe	diaspro	jaspe
jeweller	Juwelier	bijoutier	gioielliere	joyero/a
jewellery store	Juwelier	bijouterie	gioielleria	joyería
moonstone	Mondstein	adulaire	pietra di luna	tipo de opolo a feldspato
mother-of-pearl	Perlmut	nacre	madreperla	madreperla/nácar
pearl	Perle	perle	perla	perla
peridot	Peridot	péridot	peridoto	peridoto
pink	rosa	rose	rosa	rosado/rosa
platinum	Platin	platine	platino	platino
quartz	Quarz	quartz	quarzo	cuarzo
red	rot	rouge	rosso	rojo
rock crystal	Bergkristall	crystal de roche	cristallo di roccia	crystal de roca
ruby	Rubin	rubis	rubino	rubí
sapphire	Saphir	saphir	zaffiro	zafiro
silver	Silber	argent	argento	plata
topaz	Topas	topaze	topazio	topacio
tourmaline	Turmalin	tourmaline	tormalina	turmalina
turquoise	Türkis	turquoise	turchese	turquesa
white	weiß	blanc	bianco	blanco
yellow	gelb	jaune	giallo	amarillo
zircon	Zirkon	zircon	zircone	zircón

Appendix 5 – Tanzanite Values

Courtesy of the Tanzanite Foundation

COLOUR		CLARITY	CUT
Violetish **BLUE**	*Bluish* **VIOLET**		
vBE Violetish **Blue** Exceptional	**bVE** Bluish **Violet** Exceptional	**EC** Eye Clean	Excellent
vBV Violetish **Blue** Vivid	**bVV** Bluish **Violet** Vivid	**SI** Slightly Included	Very Good
vBI Violetish **Blue** Intense	**bVI** Bluish **Violet** Intense	**MI** Moderately Included	Good
vBM Violetish **Blue** Moderate	**bVM** Bluish **Violet** Moderate	**HI** Heavily Included	Fair
vBL Violetish **Blue** Light	**bVL** Bluish **Violet** Light		
vBP Violetish **Blue** Pale	**bVP** Bluish **Violet** Pale		

Note: In the rare circumstance that intensity of color exceeds the Exceptional grade, it will be graded **Exceptional** [+]

Appendix 6 – Diamond Values

Colour	Clarity						
	FL	VVS	VS	SI	I-1	I-2	I-3
D, E	100%	70%	50%	30%	25%	20%	15%
F, G	80%	65%	45%	27%	20%	18%	13%
H	65%	45%	35%	25%	18%	15%	12%
I, J	50%	35%	30%	17%	15%	12%	11%
K, L	40%	25%	20%	15%	12%	11%	10%
M, N	35%	20%	17%	14%	11%	9%	9%
O, P	30%	18%	15%	13%	9%	8%	6%
Q, R	25%	15%	13%	11%	8%	6%	4%
S - Z	15%	13%	11%	9%	6%	4%	3%

This chart demonstrates how the value of a 1 carat diamond depreciates according to colour and clarity. For example, a J colour stone with clarity classed at SI is worth only 17% of the value of a flawless D stone.

Appendix 7 – Comparative Gem Values

The following charts are designed to give an indication of the comparative value of the most important gemstones covered by this book.

The gems are listed in order of approximate value, from the lowest price per carat up to the most expensive. It is inadvisable, if not impossible, to give the actual monetary value of stones as prices fluctuate greatly due to supply and demand, varying greatly depending on where the stones are purchased.

In the chart, the red bar indicates the range of price per carat of the generally available size and quality. For instance, the first column, labelled 'Modest', indicates stones costing under £100 per carat; the subsequent columns increase in steps up to approximately £5,000 per carat.

Please bear in mind that this chart is very approximate and is only intended as a guide to the comparative values of the various gemstones.

For each gem the lower end of the price range reflects quality affected by treatments (as described earlier in the book), and the higher end of the range represents untreated, natural stones that are suitable for investment. Synthetic and manufactured stones, such as rainbow quartz and mystic topaz, have been excluded as they have little intrinsic value.

Diamonds are also excluded and reference should therefore be made to Appendix 6.

Gemstone	Modest	Affordable	Special Occasion	Expensive	Sky's the Limit
Labradorite	■				
Topaz - Blue & Green	■				
Beryl - Green	■				
Citrine	■				
Amethyst	■				
Danburite	■				
Almandine Garnet	■				
Moonstone	■				
Pyrope Garnet	■				
Kunzite	■				
Beryl - Yellow	■				
Sapphire - White	■				
Iolite	■				
Fire Opal	■				
Spessartine Garnet	■				

Gemstone	Modest	Affordable	Special Occasion	Expensive	Sky's the Limit
Beryl - Morganite					
Andalusite					
Rhodolite Garnet					
Tourmaline - Yellow					
Peridot					
Aquamarine					
Zircon - Blue					
Chrysoberyl - Yellow					
Tourmaline - Red					
Sapphire - Green					
Opal - White					
Sapphire - Yellow					
Tanzanite					
Topaz - Pink					
Topaz - Imperial					
Tourmaline - Green					
Spinel - Blue					
Spinel - Red					
Sapphire - Star					
Sapphire - Pink					
Benitoite					
Sapphire Padparadsha					
Tourmaline - Blue					
Chrysoberyl - Cats Eye					
Demantoid - Garnet					
Opal - Black					>
Ruby - Star					>
Sapphire - Blue					>
Alexandrite					>
Emerald					>
Tourmaline - Paraiba					>
Ruby					>

Appendix 8 – Further Reading

If you would like to develop your interest in the study of gemstones, the following books are suggested reading:

Balfour, I., (1997), *Famous Diamonds*, Christie's Books, London

Bennet & Mascetti, (2003), *Understanding Jewellery*. Antique Collectors' Club, Woodbridge

Campbell-Pederson, M., (2004), *Gem & Ornamental Materials of Organic Origin*. Elsevier Ltd., Oxford

Kunz, G. F., (1989), *The Curious Lore of Precious Stones*. Bell Publishing Co., New York

Pickford, I., (Ed.), (1989), *Jackson's Silver & Gold Marks of England, Scotland & Ireland*, Antique Collectors' Club, Woodbridge

Read, P. J., (1999), *Gemmology*, 3rd Edition. Elsevier Ltd., Oxford

Tanenbaum, C., (2006), *Vintage Costume Jewellery*, Antique Collectors' Club, Woodbridge

Webster, R., (1998) *Gemmologists' Compendium*. Robert Hale Ltd., London

For details of courses in Gemmology please contact:

Gem-A,
27 Greville Street,
London EC1N 8TN

Gem-A also has Allied Teaching Centres in the following places:

Belgium	Hong Kong	Myanmar	Sweden
Canada	India	Netherlands	Taiwan
China	Italy	New Zealand	Thailand
Finland	Japan	Norway	U.S.A.
France	Korea	Singapore	
Greece	Madagascar	Sri Lanka	

For contact details, please visit the Gem-A website:
www.gem-a.info

Index